In this book, you'll meet a person who seems surprised by the mystery of his life and who invites you to join him on a journey of exploration. Along the way, you'll learn about the early days of the tech sector in America, you'll experience something of what it was to be a Jew in midcentury America, and you will, above all, delight in the person of the author.
—*Tom Cox, Former Deputy Mayor, City of Pittsburgh*

Rarely does one get an up-close view of a journey that leads to wisdom embedded in a passion for nurturing innovation. Jack Roseman tells a story both provocative and charming, all the while reminding us that the conquest of fear can produce great beauty.
—*Audrey Russo, President & CEO, Pittsburgh Technology Council*

To: Sue—
A great friend whom
I love dearly —

Jack
Roseman

Jump!

How I Rose from Poverty and Anti-Semitism to Become a Tech Sector Pioneer and a *Mensch*

By Jack Roseman with Evan Pattak

DEDICATION

This book is dedicated to my wife, friend and companion of the last 57 years. What I have accomplished during those years is largely due to Judy. When I needed encouragement, she was there; when I needed a kick, she was there, and when I needed some loving, she was there.

Sure am a lucky guy!

CONTENTS

FOREWORD

ALWAYS WITH HUMOR,
ALWAYS WITH HUMAN DECENCY

This is a book about the making of a *mensch*. You might wonder how a little brown woman raised a Hindu in India, learning to speak English only after seventh grade and not meeting a Jew until years later when she started running her own business, even knows what a *mensch* might be. Well, some matches, they say, are made in heaven. I believe the best ones are made right here on earth. As was mine with Jack Roseman.

I met Jack when I came to Carnegie Mellon University in Pittsburgh to complete my MBA (actually MSIA as they called it then) and Ph.D. Jack was teaching at the Entrepreneurship Center there and I began working as a teaching assistant for the TEMP (The Entrepreneurial Management Program) course he taught for growth-aspiring entrepreneurs in the Three Rivers area. I made the slides for his lectures. And as I sat in the back of the room, every once in a while, a participant in the program would turn incredulously to me or to another participant to exclaim, "Is this guy for real?"

That usually meant that Jack had said something about what it takes to bring key people on board and motivate them to deliver beyond not only their expectations as leaders of their firms, but also beyond their own expectations of themselves. As Jack was wont to mention, "it is easy to hire and motivate people who will deliver 9-to-5. It is the 5-to-9 that matters more." In other words, most of what you learn in good management courses will teach you how to hire good people and motivate them to do the jobs they are hired for. What makes great entrepreneurial leadership is to get people mentally and emotionally engaged when they are not supposed to, like when they are at the mall or in the shower. How do you get people to want to think about ideas that can grow the company, fix problems before they occur and even see the world through the well-being of the organization as a whole above and beyond any job description the best headhunter in the world can come up with? The key to that is being a *mensch* and building the kind of venture that would value, nurture and help a *mensch* flourish.

To do that, Jack offers a variety of techniques you can practice every day, from walking around and pouring coffee for your employees to looking them straight in the eye during tough times—always with humor, humility and authenticity — to continuously learning and improving not only your venture, but also yourself as a human being. In the years I have known Jack, I have seen him interact with people of every ilk — students, successful entrepreneurs, family and friends in distress. He is always willing to listen, even to arrogant jerks, so long as he can learn from them. He will listen carefully to upstart students like me quarreling with him on things he has truly learned in the trenches, go away to think about it and come back with penetrating and difficult questions that would make both of us rethink our premises. But always, always with humor and the human decency of a true *mensch*.

What is a true *mensch*? In India we have a word for a sense and sensibility that goes beyond "knowing" and "feeling." The word is *rasa*, and it means something like a flavor, a flair, a taste, a felt experience that can be captured neither in the cerebral nor the sensual, yet can straddle both. The "truth" of Jack's definition of *mensch* lies in the life he has led and the lives he has touched. As I mentioned before, what I have with Jack is a match made here on earth. The love we share is that of family, friend, flirt and even worthwhile foe all rolled into one. It is the kind of love only a *mensch* could earn and nourish!

Truth be told, even now, I'm not sure I know what a *mensch* actually is. But through my years with Jack, I have developed a *rasa* for *menschness*. And so will you, as you read this delightful book. And in the process, you also will learn what it takes to become a successful entrepreneur, an inspiring leader and someone capable of designing the "good" life in all its meanings, for yourself as well as for others around you.

Saras Sarasvathy
Isidore Horween Research Professor, The Darden School
University of Virginia

1. IN ROVNO

Ukraine long has been a geographic and political prize in the wars of Europe, the sort of place where it was a good idea to keep multiple flags in your closet because you never were sure which country was the ruler *du jour*. It was part of Russia before the Bolshevik Revolution, then was controlled at various times by German, Ukrainian, Bolshevik and Polish forces. Between the world wars, it was part of Poland, much the worse for it when Germany overran Poland. Even today, Ukraine is struggling to retain its independence in the face of Russian threats.

As an important Ukrainian town, Rovno (now known as Rivne) experienced all this buffeting yet managed to support a Jewish community that, in 1940, was estimated at 25,000, roughly half the town's entire population. Among Rovno's Jews were Bessie Guz Roseman and Abraham Roseman, my parents. I was born Yonkil Roseman in 1931 in Lynn, MA, where my parents settled after they immigrated. I know little of their lives in Rovno, except that my father was a tailor and my parents already had three children in Rovno — my brothers Leibel and Hyman and my sister Lena — and that my mother had two sisters.

Once in America, they seldom mentioned the Old Country, a reticence I've noticed on the part of other immigrants. The Old Country is dead to them; they want to speak only of their new beginnings and possibilities rather than dwell on the harsh past. Then, too, they want to be perceived as patriotic Americans, not would-be saboteurs carrying the torch for their homelands.

In Rovno, my parents may have grown and produced as much of their own food as they could. On several occasions, when times were particularly tough for us in Lynn, my mother lamented: "I should have stayed in Rovno. At least we had a cow." Given the events that occurred in Rovno after she left, I'm sure these were just moments of frustration for her and not genuine regrets.

In any case, I know they were dirt poor in Rovno and victimized by anti-Semitism. My mother well remembered the times the Cossack hordes stormed into Rovno and ripped the earrings from Jewish women and girls — even more painful than it sounds since the women of that era typically pierced their ears. Poverty and anti-Semitism were the twin drivers in their immigration to America; as so many others, the Roseman family had a plan.

My father would come first, settling with his brother Louis in Boston. Then, as he saved enough money to pay for the trip, he would send for each member of the family.

Abraham landed in the mid-1920s, although he didn't stay long in Boston with either brother, settling instead in Lynn, about eight miles north of Boston. Next, in 1930, came my mother with Hymie. Lena made the trip alone in 1934 when she was 13. I can't say if Lena was mature for her age, but she likely grew up fast on that transatlantic journey — alone and seasick throughout — and that was only part of it. An equally uncertain trip — from Ellis Island to Boston — still lay ahead.

Fortunately, she was aided by a Jewish settlement agency that got her on a train and instructed a skycap to make sure she got off in Boston. Pretty iffy, especially for a 13-year-old immigrant traveling alone.

"I was afraid they would forget me, and I would end up in the wrong city," she once told me. "And there I would have been, speaking not a word of English."

I used to tease her about it: "What are you complaining about? You got a free cruise." For some reason, she never saw the humor in that.

That left only Leibel who, by the late 1930s, was a grown man with a wife and two children. But money to finance Leibel's exodus was harder to come by than it once was for my father, who now had with him a family of five to shelter, feed and clothe. Plus, if Leibel were to bring his family, the cost would skyrocket. My parents were making progress and staying in touch with Leibel by letter. Finally, they had enough money saved to finance passage to America for Leibel and his family, and they communicated the good news. Neither that letter, nor any subsequent correspondence to Leibel, was answered. My mother's letters to her sisters? Also unanswered. My parents were frantic with concern that was very much justified.

We know now that, as part of the conquest of Poland, the Nazis occupied Ukraine, including Rovno. Their plan for Rovno's Jews was simple—eliminate them. They did this in two great waves. In November 1941, the Germans marched more than 15,000 Jews to a pine grove in Sosenki Forest on the pretext of giving them new work assignments. There, the Jews were shot — only one bullet per Jew was the Nazi practice, since Jews weren't worth more than that.

The town's remaining Jews, still more than 5,000, were herded into a ghetto, where they were left to eke out a meager existence . . . but not for long. In December 1942, Rovno's remaining Jews were forced onto rail cars and taken to the forest near Kostopol, about 40 miles north of Rovno, where the Nazis executed them. The roundup was particularly brutal; according to testimony at the Nuremberg trials, many who resisted were beaten or shot. Even the dead were dumped into rail cars and transported to the forest so they could be incinerated with those about to die.

We never were able to confirm the details of the deaths of Leibel, his family and my two aunts and their families. My parents learned of the Rovno massacres largely through word of mouth, though I imagine they discovered the scope of the killings through *The Forward*, the Yiddish-language daily they often read.

I can't begin to describe for you the sense of loss I feel for the brother I never met . . . and never would meet. I often wondered: with the age difference between us, what would our relationship have been? Would Leibel have been my friend? My mentor? I never would know. And if my loss was great, imagine the impact on my mother. She'd lost her first-born son, her grandchildren, her sisters and her sisters' children.

Emptiness. Outrage. Powerlessness — we felt them all. Leibel's death, and the deliberate brutality of it, cast a long shadow over the Rosemans as we tried to make a life in America.

* * * * *

In Rovno, now a bustling city of about 250,000 inhabitants, a memorial stands to commemorate the killing of the town's Jews by the Nazis. For me, that's not personal enough. I was — and still am — tormented by Leibel's death and the Holocaust itself. I know others — Jews and Gentiles alike — share the same grief and anger, and I wanted to find some way to express those emotions and provide a fitting memorial for all the victims and serve as a reminder that we could not let such a thing happen again.

A few years ago, I was introduced to Michael Kraus, a talented sculptor and fellow congregant at Temple Ohav

Shalom in Pittsburgh's North Hills, where my family worships. The temple had been planning a Holocaust memorial, and I agreed to underwrite the work Michael would design, sculpt and install. The initial sketches Michael shared with me didn't evoke a sense of horror. I challenged him:

"If you insist on this design, be my guest. But I think you could do better. Create something that people will go out of their way to see. Create something that will hit them in the heart."

The statue he ultimately designed and crafted, which now stands in the temple's Holocaust Memorial Garden, is vastly different. We see a man, face invisible, hooded by his *tallit*, his prayer shawl. His shoulders are bent, perhaps in prayer, perhaps in pain. The *tzitzit*, the fringes of the *tallit* that emerge from his sleeves, aren't made of cloth. They're barbed wire, much like manacles, suggesting the fences enclosing Nazi concentration camps. It's stark, moving and unforgettable. Once when I was contemplating the memorial, the shadows and light were wavering in such a way that I imagined I saw silhouettes of Nazis on the temple walls. I felt my eyes tearing.

He hit me in the heart.

2. "YONKIL, KNOW YOUR CUSTOMER"

"Lynn, Lynn, the City of Sin," was the rhyme that acknowledged and poked fun at Lynn's growing reputation as a haven for vice. But as Lynn, swollen by immigrants like the Rosemans, grew to a population of more than 100,000 by 1930, it might more accurately have been called "The City of Shoes." In the early 20th century, the town was home to more than 100 shoe manufacturing companies that produced an estimated 15 million pairs of shoes each year. These factories attracted immigrants with "needle skills," since shoes at that time were hand made. My father wasn't a shoemaker, of course, but his tailoring skills made him a natural for Lynn.

In those days, Jewish immigrants often followed a progression, clawing out a living in hardscrabble neighborhoods such as Boston's West End and North End, saving enough money to move to more comfortable homes in better neighborhoods, including Roxbury and Dorchester. The Rosemans followed a progression as well. We moved from a terrible neighborhood to a bad neighborhood and stayed there for several decades.

Our home on Summer Circle was a rental in a six-unit building; we were on the second floor, one of two Jewish families in the building. This was not a typical Jewish ghetto neighborhood; indeed, Lynn already was a gritty mix of poverty, with African-Americans outnumbering whites and many other ethnic groups represented. We had a neighbor on Summer Circle who took great pains to explain that he was Assyrian, not Syrian. He was a nice guy — he was the local representative for General Motors — but I had no idea what an Assyrian was.

We had five rooms: a kitchen, a parlor and three bedrooms — one for my parents, one for Lena, the third for Hy and me. My brother and I not only shared a room, but we also slept in the same bed until Hy left for college. Our room also housed a small radio, which was not the great source of entertainment and togetherness you often see depicted in pictures of Depression-era family life. The apartment boasted a unique central heating system. It was called "the stove," and it was our only source of heat. Because of the way the apartment was configured, no heat reached Lena's room. She froze during the harsh New England winters, but she never complained. I remember leaving Hy on cold winter nights to sleep on the floor near the stove — anything for a little warmth. There was a bathtub, but my mother bathed me in a big basin with water she heated on the stove.

My mother kept our apartment spotless, but she couldn't do much about the rats that patrolled the spaces between our building and the neighboring structures. As a toddler, I once got upset because I couldn't find my milk bottle. My mother took me to the window and pointed down at the rats.

"See that big black and brown one? He stole your bottle."

When they first arrived, none of the Rosemans knew a word of English, so we spoke Yiddish exclusively. I was born in 1931, a year after my mother arrived with Hy, and even though my parents, Hy and Lena had picked up some English, we still spoke Yiddish in the house. We were a curious bunch, trying to Americanize while clinging to Old World notions.

For example: My mother and father were both extremely superstitious. My mother believed in the "Evil Eye;" I'm not sure if she tried to cast its spell from time to time, but I know she believed in its power. She also was a practitioner of home healing and used modern medicine sparingly — understandable, since a visit to the doctor cost $2, a princely sum for us. When one of the children was sick — a frequent occurrence in the chilly apartment — she would treat us with *bankes*, vacuum cups that, she believed, when placed on our backs would draw off fever.

My father warned us never to look out a window at night; what he thought we might see there never was clear to me. If an insect flew into the apartment, he would stalk it, trap it in a sieve and release it outside. "What God makes, you should not kill," he would say, though I guess this was more faith than superstition. With my father, the two were hard to separate.

He refused to discard the clippings from his fingernails and toenails. "If you toss them out and someone steps on them, it's bad luck for you," he would say. So he meticulously gathered his clippings, wrapped them in tissue and inserted them in cracks in the basement wall. This never became an issue with our fellow tenants since the basement was partitioned. In our little section, the tissues, peeking out here and there, made an interesting mosaic.

*   *   *   *   *

My mother was a spitfire. Given her circumstances — recent immigrant; son, sisters and grandchildren massacred by Nazis; no command of English; husband who didn't work for most of the year; family of five to manage — she had to be a spitfire to make it, and to allow all of us to make it. She was attractive in a no-nonsense way, sturdily built, and when she wore her hair up, you could see determination etched on her brow.

As I mentioned, we spoke Yiddish in the house, which didn't help my mother learn English. At times, she was as helpless in the new language as I was. One time she sent me to the store for a can of "shit beans."

"Ma, I don't think . . . "

"Just tell them at the store. They'll know."

Ever the dutiful son, I repeated my mother's instructions to the clerk. To my everlasting relief, he brought out a can of chickpeas, which seemed a helluva lot more appetizing to me than shit beans.

But she picked up English, bit by bit, even teaching herself fractions, an achievement that filled her with as much pride as becoming a U.S. citizen. (Achieving citizenship may have been her proudest moment. She enjoyed learning about America's governmental units, and she dutifully listened to the radio shows of Kate Smith who, her citizenship instructor advised, had "perfect enunciation.") At first, I couldn't imagine why she had chosen this arcane math skill to master, but I learned anew its value each time she took me shopping with her. She would point a finger at me and sternly say, "Yonkil, know your customer." Then we would leave for, say, the furniture store, where the poor, unsuspecting merchant had no idea Hurricane Bessie was churning just offshore.

First, she would ask to see the owner. When that unwitting fellow arrived, she would finger the price tag on her desired item, making sure the owner could see the tag.

"These prices are for rich people," she'd say. "What are you going to charge me?"

She usually got the deal she wanted. She may have been superstitious and Old Country, but she was a first-class negotiator.

My father's income wouldn't keep a family of five, so my

mother found herself in such negotiations all the time. When haggling wasn't possible, she went to other extremes, *schlepping* all the way across town if she could score modest savings.

"Yonkil," she told me many times, "I just walked an extra mile to save a penny. A penny! Tell me: What did you do today?"

I was just a kid — what was I supposed to answer? I played today, Ma. Play in her view was a waste of time. Over the years, I'm afraid, that came to be my view as well: If I'm not working, I'm wasting my life, so I must work.

Another time, she was sitting on our couch, not looking well, and I knew she was feeling ill. She opened her pocketbook.

"Yonkil, I have $2. I can go to the doctor, or I can buy groceries. Which shall I do?"

She opted for groceries, and I felt terrible that she had to make that choice. But I also knew that making me feel terrible was part of the plan. She knew how to press the guilt button, and it was something that inevitably helped shape me.

She did not show affection to any of her children, never praised or encouraged us. I suppose these days some would call it "tough love." If I cried as a child, she refused to comfort me. Instead, she looked at me reprovingly.

"Stop *pishing mit die eigen*," she'd say. Stop pissing with your eyes. Tough love, indeed.

If she ever showed any warmth to her children, Hy was usually the object. My brother overcame polio, scarlet fever and diphtheria — he suffered them all simultaneously — and even my mother's heart was moved by his strength. This, of course, did not go unnoticed by Hy's bedmate.

"Ma," I asked her once, "who do you love better, Hy or me?"

I was looking for some small display of affection, some reassurance. But she got all Solomonic on me.

She held up two fingers.

"If I lose this finger, I'll miss it. If I lose this other finger, I'll miss it just as much. I love all my fingers equally."

I walked away, feeling I'd been had, still convinced she loved Hy more.

I did get the better of her once, or at least it seemed that way at the time. I asked her for money for an ice cream cone. To my utter surprise she said: "There's a penny in my pocketbook. Take it and buy your ice cream."

This was unprecedented, and I wasn't waiting for a second invitation. I opened her pocketbook and found not one penny, but two. I got to thinking how good a double-decker cone would taste. I'd never had one, and this surely would be my only chance. So I took both pennies and bought my double-decker. The sweet cream burned my tongue. I felt guilty, ashamed of stealing a penny from my mother, the one she had walked an extra mile to save. Truly, I'm ashamed of it to this day.

I often wonder if my mother would have been more loving, more demonstrative, at least, if she hadn't lost Leibel, her grandchildren and her sisters. Through the war years, she cried for them just about every afternoon. But I think, ultimately, she was who she was — a formidable, austere person — and nothing would have changed that.

As strained as our relationship was when I was a child, that's how close we became in later years. We'd both matured, and we had, after all, endured some common challenges — learning English, surviving poverty — under the same roof.

After my father died, I used to send her plane tickets so she could visit my wife Judy and me and the kids wherever we were living at the time. She got her first plane ride that way, a thrilling and bewildering experience for her. For one of these trips, I phoned to tell her I was sending her a ticket. I didn't choose my words carefully enough.

"I'm sending you a ticket, Ma. You'll fly here on a jet."

"Yonkil," she said, "I know how to travel on a plane. I don't know how to travel on a jet."

And no matter how hard I tried to persuade her that planes and jets were one and the same, for the longest time, she would not travel on anything called a jet.

My parents eventually moved to a better neighborhood in Lynn, but I knew times were still tough for Ma without my father's modest income to help. So I sent her money, often $1,000, each month. I should have known she was doing the fractions and coming up with a plan.

"Yonkil," she said. "I want to give you $1,000, and you'll invest it for me."

How could I possibly explain market risks in a way she would understand? I didn't want to repeat my "jet" blunder.

"Let's say I invest your $1,000, and it does well, so I give you back $2,000. What then?"

She thought a minute.

"Well, I'll give you the $2,000. You'll invest it and give me back $4,000."

As usual, there was no arguing with her impeccable logic and math skills.

The more I thought about this, the more it pleased me. For perhaps the first time in her life, she was expressing complete trust and confidence in my abilities and judgment. Would that she had done that decades sooner.

*   *   *   *   *

My mother cast a large shadow, even over her husband, the presumptive head of the household. He left most of the budgeting, spending and child rearing to her, seldom engaging in arguments he knew he couldn't win. He did insist that we practice our penmanship, so that Hy and I developed beautiful handwriting. But there was one position he held firm, one from which he would not budge.

For tailors, the market rate in those days was $12 per week. My father refused to work for a penny less than $14. The big clothing store in our area was Kennedy's, which was paying its tailors the standard $12 a week. But around the Christmas and Easter holidays, when business was heaviest, Kennedy's increased the weekly rate to $14. For much of my childhood, those were the only times my father would work. That's where he drew his line in the sand.

"We'll all starve first," he would say. That might well have been prophetic but for my mother's insistence that Lena forego high school to work and supplement the family income. Without the money Lena brought home from the dress factory, we might well have starved. We could have sought aid from a Jewish relief agency, but my mother never would have admitted she needed charity or accepted it if offered.

Our situation improved somewhat during World War II when my father got a full-time job as a janitor at the Navy yard at Charlestown. The work went well enough, although he was plagued by a persistent anti-Semite, a fellow janitor who always called him a "fucking Jew." My father solved that problem with a lead pipe.

"You sonovabitch," he told his tormentor. "Because of you, I'll probably spend the rest of my life in jail because if you call me that one more time, I'm gonna hit you over the head with this pipe."

My father may have been mild mannered, but when he drew a line, you'd better not cross it. The verbal abuse stopped forthwith.

My brother also found work, at the General Electric plant in Lynn. In those days, you could ride the bus from Summer Street to GE. My job was to meet Hy at the bus stop in wintertime and make sure he didn't slip on the ice on the way home, a possibility we all feared because of his bad leg.

The extra money guaranteed that we would eat — beef, even, although we never could be sure which part of the cow my mother would serve. One of her favorite dishes was *kishka*, stuffed cow intestine, which she would routinely overcook. I developed a taste for it and to this day enjoy a hearty helping of well-done *kishka*. On occasion, we even ate *lungen*, the lungs. My mother sometimes tossed the lungs to the dog, which made me wonder if we were eating dog food. In recent years, the federal government outlawed the serving of animal lungs for human consumption because lungs can be contaminated during the slaughtering process. We didn't know that then. We ate *lungen* and didn't seem the worse for it.

* * * *

With such a sporadic work schedule (before World War II), my father had a lot of time on his hands. He spent much of that in the basement, where he assembled collections of many things — even beyond his growing cache of toenail clippings. Summers were unbearably hot in the basement. Moreover, my father walked with a noticeable limp, the result of a childhood accident that broke the arch in his foot. When he logged countless flights of steps on those steamy days, his shirt would be soaked with sweat.

His glory was the *shul* he and some friends created in a converted residence near Summer Circle. It was a smallish house, so you know the congregation didn't have many members. My father was the *shul's* vice president. During Passover, he would sweep each windowsill, symbolically wiping away any crumbs of *chometz*, food not kosher for Passover. My favorite holiday was *Simchas Torah*, a harvest festival following the High Holidays that also celebrates the completion of the annual cycle of *Torah* readings. That was an especially joyful holiday at our house and *shul*.

On *Shabbos*, he would be in *shul* much of the day. He and his *minyan*, the 10 adult males required for many Jewish rituals, would pray, then celebrate the Sabbath by drinking cheap whiskey. He always drank two glasses — never one, never three. He'd come home twinkling.

I occasionally walked to *shul* with him on Saturdays. That was really the only time we could talk as father and son, since the Dictator couldn't hear us. I could tell him whatever was on my mind, no matter how frivolous. I remember one time I had listened the day before to *The Shadow* — remember? *Who knows what evil lurks in the hearts of men? The shadow knows.* So I told him all about the latest installment. In retrospect, I imagine he was bored stiff, but he listened patiently and asked questions. It induced me to talk some more. I always knew I was my father's favorite. Lord knows I needed to be somebody's favorite.

*   *   *   *   *

Lena was 10 years older than I, working in the dress factory when I was still a kid, married several years thereafter. So I don't remember her being around much. She always was kind, generous and uncomplaining, even though the meager warmth from our "central heating" never reached her bedroom. She even taught me to foxtrot when, for some reason, I thought not knowing how to dance was a serious omission in my education. When we were adults, she did share with me her one childhood complaint.

"In all those years I gave Ma the money I earned —every Friday I gave it to her — she never once said 'thank you.'"

However, Hy and I became very close. He made an amazing, courageous comeback from those childhood diseases, although he emerged from them with one bum leg and a diminished sense of hearing. He walked with crutches for years before graduating to a cane. When he heard that Franklin Delano Roosevelt, himself a polio victim, had purchased a facility in Georgia called Warm Springs for treatment of the disease, he wrote directly to FDR to seek admission. He didn't get in, but he didn't let that stop him. He learned to swim. (I never did.) He joined the Boy Scouts. When they went hiking, he went hiking, never letting his crutches or braces stop him.

He played violin excellently and painted, and I know he never had lessons. How could we have afforded those? He was extremely handsome, reminding everyone of Liberace. Plus, he had bulging biceps built up from walking with crutches. Liberace may have had Hy's pompadour, but I assure you, Liberace never had those guns. Hy earned his master's degree in bacteriology from the University of Massachusetts and worked most of his career as a high school math and physics teacher.

He loved science and read many science texts. What he learned he taught to me, even though we were kids, giving me informal instruction in geography, geology, archaeology, anthropology, all of which helped steer me to math and the sciences.

Hy was my hero, my Superman. One day, when we were walking home from the movies, we encountered a snarling German shepherd who seemed intent on dismembering us, at the very least. Hy shoved me behind him, so that I was shielded by his body. He raised his cane and shook it menacingly at the dog, which, to my relief, took the hint and ran off. So when I say he was my hero, that's no exaggeration.

Despite his considerable accomplishments, I learned he suffered from the same inferiority complex that afflicted us all. I was in high school when he sat me down beside him.

"There are very few Rosemans in this country," he said, "and look at us: me with a bum leg, your father the same, your sister never even in high school. If the name Roseman is ever to mean something, it's up to you."

This was too much for me. Here was my brother, my Superman, telling me he never would amount to anything, and that I, his inferior in most ways, must carry the family flag. Hy was putting a ton of bricks on my shoulders and I felt, not for the first or last time, weighed down by the task. I sobbed when he was finished, and I couldn't stop sobbing.

*   *   *   *   *

It was a bleak childhood, but we did have some forms of entertainment. Every so often on a Saturday, Hy and I walked into downtown Lynn to the Auditorium Theatre, where we could enjoy a double feature for 10 cents. The theater frequently offered horror movies like *The Mummy*, which I found enjoyable but seldom terribly frightening. I was surprised years later when Hy confessed that these movies scared him to the point where he was actually gratified that we shared a bed; my presence helped him overcome his agitation and fall asleep. Oh well. Even Superman had his kryptonite.

My mother, unrelenting as she was, loved to slip away for an afternoon of bingo or penny-ante poker. In retrospect, I don't blame her for seeking a little time off. Back then, though, I was terrified by what might happen.

"Isn't there a chance you'll lose that money?" I said.

She fixed me with one of her famous steely glares.

"I don't lose at bingo."

If that's true, I thought, I wonder why you don't go more often. I didn't dare say it aloud.

When we bought our first television, she surprised me again by religiously watching *Toast of the Town*, which became more famous by its later name, *The Ed Sullivan Show*. I was honored when she invited me to watch with her.

I joined her in the middle of a Sullivan show once to find her in a state of great excitement.

"Yonkil, would you believe they have a new sponsor for Sullivan?"

"Who is it?"

"It's Kotex."

This was not an era when people spoke freely of female genitalia and menstruation, so I expressed my doubts.

"Watch. You'll see."

So I watched with her. Sure enough, there was a new advertisement. It showed beautiful people happily snapping photographs.

"Ma," I said. "Kodak, not Kotex."

Christmas was a time of great joy for us — unusual for a family of Conservative Jews, perhaps, but Christmas always was something special for my father. He loved to show me Christmas photos in magazines. When the store windows were decked out for the holiday, we would go *spatzieren*, walking around town to admire the store windows. My father was transfixed by sleighs, as if imagining himself gliding over the river and through the woods, far away from his difficult life. For me, the best part of those displays was the miniature trains going round and round. I wished many times I could have a set. Never did get one, though, years later, my parents did buy me a $10 used bicycle.

I believed in Santa Claus — my parents never discouraged it — and we did encounter Santa of a sort. When my father worked at Kennedy's during the Christmas season, his manager gave him a bonus — gifts to take home to his kids. I was pretty excited one Christmas morning to open my coloring book, only to find that all the figures were colored in. Rather than spend a nickel, his manager had re-gifted items his own kids already had used.

A coloring book already colored in. If there's anything that symbolizes my childhood, that's it.

By far our most lively entertainment occurred Saturday evenings when my parents often hosted what turned out to be an informal discussion group of neighbors, family and friends. A neighbor, a woman from Poland who actually owned her own house on Summer Circle, often took part, as did another neighbor who was a *shamas*, an official who manages the day-to-day maintenance of a synagogue. When Lena married, her father-in-law — also a *shamas* —

frequently was there. Then there was our neighbor Kramer, a soft goods purveyor who definitely was not a *shamas*; he was a devout Communist who wasn't afraid to let you know it. And of course, there were my mother, as opinionated as any of them, and my father, still in the glow of his two *Shabbos* whiskeys.

Our kitchen those nights was like an early template for the United Nations, which still was several years away from formation. A discussion might begin in Yiddish, with sidebar conversations in Russian and Polish and the occasional English expression spooned in for flavor.

I loved listening to them. They were passionate, funny and sure they were right as they solved the world's problems. They concluded, for example, that when 95 percent of Americans were employed, the American government deliberately and misleadingly called it "full employment." Why? Because the government didn't really need full employment. If we ever had that, employers would lose the ability to fire their workers, since there would be no unemployed people to replace them. Thus, the term "full employment" was a government hoax to aid big companies.

An early conspiracy theory hatched in the Rosemans' kitchen.

*   *   *   *   *

School should have been an oasis for me, an escape from the tension and poverty of home, but it turned out to be one more circle of hell — hell at home, hell on the streets and now hell at school. Why? On the day I should have started first grade at Washington Elementary, I spoke little English. Children in that situation today might be given a battery of tests to determine their abilities and needs. They might be offered tutoring in the English language. The school district, possibly in association with my parents, had a simpler plan for me. They concluded I was dim-witted and held me out of school for a year.

I don't know what they thought this would accomplish, as I was still speaking and hearing only Yiddish at home. Perhaps they wanted to protect me a little longer from the horrors they were sure awaited me at school. Lord knows the neighborhood streets gave them plenty to worry about. One of the kids who lived in our building used to steal food stamps and distribute them to his pals. The older kids liked to break into bakeries; sometimes, they gave the little kids stolen pastries. When those older kids played Cowboys & Indians, they used real BB guns. Neither the school district nor my parents could keep me from that forever. I started first grade at the age of 7 rather than the customary 6, already stamped a slow learner.

This diagnosis affected my training in *cheder*, Hebrew school, as well. Hy and Lena learned to speak Hebrew, but my parents didn't want to "strain my brain" with such an arduous task. Only for my Bar Mitzvah, a decidedly low-key affair in deference to the ongoing war, was I permitted to read in Hebrew.

School was excruciatingly difficult. I was picking up English as I could, but it didn't help me much with lengthy reading assignments. I gravitated naturally to math, which uses a sort of universal language and has a lighter reading load. In fact, math was the only subject to which I really paid attention.

Here's how I got by. Apart from math assignments, I rarely did homework in the other subjects. Instead, the day before a test in one of those subjects, I skipped school, staying home to study for the test, as best I could, in our heavily trafficked bathroom, the only place in our apartment where

I could be alone. My high school physics teacher actually tumbled to my strategy. He noticed I was absent one day and told the class: "Roseman must have a test tomorrow."

Even if I'd had the aptitude and interest in those other subjects, I wouldn't have had much time to devote to them; our poverty forced me to work wherever I could find it. I sold newspapers. Shined shoes on street corners. Babysat. Shoveled snow in the winter. Worked throughout high school as counter help in Mr. Brody's pharmacy just down the street from Summer Circle. Flicked chickens. (Chicken-flicking is the fine art of removing feathers from dead chickens, a service so valuable to butchers that they paid 10 cents per chicken flicked.) I didn't know it at that time, but chicken flicking would not be my only experience in the culinary arts — and not my worst encounter with dead poultry.

While I was compiling such an impressive resume, I managed to get by with middling grades. It didn't matter, I told myself, because one day I would become president of General Motors. I'm not sure why I chose this particularly fantasy, except that GM was a brand that virtually everyone knew and respected. Each time I struggled with yet another reading assignment, I knew I would show them all the true Roseman someday and fulfill Hy's expectations of me.

*　　*　　*　　*　　*

Yet another horror of school was anti-Semitism so routine and regular that you came to expect it. In Boston, just eight miles south of us, we saw anti-Semitism on a grand, often violent scale, with roving gangs running wild through the city as they attacked Jewish kids. We didn't experience anything of quite that scope in Lynn. There, hatred of Jews was institutionalized.

When I was in the first grade, I fell on the playground and scraped up my face pretty badly. The teacher, Mrs. Berry, was furious with me and refused to send me for treatment, insisting that I stay at my desk for the rest of the day. My wounds became infected and so covered by layers of pimples that my father swore he didn't recognize me when he first saw me. I needed regular treatments at a hospital to clear the infection. My father visited the principal to complain, and Mrs. Berry was duly reprimanded.

In high school, I once was heading to chemistry class when I realized I'd forgotten my notebook. A friend had an extra notebook and offered it to me. It was more a notepad, much smaller than the large notebooks we usually used. But it was the best I could come up with. In class, Mr. Hutchins was lecturing when he noticed me scribbling on the tiny pad. He looked at me with disgust.

"Why are you people always trying to save money?" he said.

Not every teacher was like that. I still remember when Miss Atwood, our fifth grade teacher, praised me to the skies for doing well on a test. I know she was trying to buck me up — and it worked, at least for a while.

But if the teachers were anti-Semitic, you can imagine how bad the students were. I had to pass a Catholic church en route to Hebrew school; it was scarier than passing a cemetery. "Christ killer!" the bullies would shout, chasing me all the way to school. The bullies at school usually got me between classes when we were moving from one floor to the other — sort of a smash-and-grab MO. Before they beat me, they always asked, "You a Jew?"

One time when I saw them coming, I thought I'd try to compromise.

"You a Jew?"

"Only one of my parents is Jewish," I responded quite reasonably.

You know what? They hit me just as hard, teaching me a painful lesson: Compromise is not the answer.

I couldn't even escape anti-Semitism at home. There, one of our downstairs neighbors, an older kid, put out a lit cigarette in the palm of my hand, a fun prank to pull on a Jewish kid.

If you add it all up, I might have been the victim of a dozen or more direct instances of anti-Semitism — that wouldn't include all the verbal slurs — perhaps not an extraordinary number when spread over an entire adolescence. But the effect on me was profound. As so many Jews who'd felt its sting, I became extremely sensitive to anti-Semitism, perceiving it where it was but also where it wasn't. Even when Gentile kids weren't bullying me and may well have meant me no harm at all, I saw a look on their faces that seemed to say, "What the fuck are you doing here?"

This feeling persisted through much of my adult life, even though I can't cite for you any specific instances of anti-Semitism in my professional career. The damage had been done. About the only time I wasn't dogged by this — I don't want to call it paranoia because some of them probably *were* out to get me — was when I visited Israel. My first time there, I was temporarily free of this sense that I could be persecuted at any minute. In Israel, I knew, if somebody didn't like me, it wasn't because I'm Jewish. Back home, though, I still wonder: Does he see me as a person or as *a Jew*?

When I get into that kind of funk, I try to remember the example of my Uncle Morris, my father's younger brother.

He was a man so filled with good humor and warmth that when he told a joke, as he frequently did, he broke up with laughter well before the punch line. He always was my champion, encouraging me and telling me how smart I was when everybody else insisted I was backward. You can imagine how much I looked forward to seeing him.

As a young man, Uncle Morris by chance heard some flute music and was so mesmerized that he persuaded a Boston musical instrument company to give him a flute — and throw in free lessons. He and his wife operated a music school from their apartment in Dorchester.

Income for a freelance flutist wasn't very secure, so he applied for a job teaching music in Boston's public schools. The manager told Uncle Morris he would hire him if he'd had an opening, but that if Uncle Morris really wanted a job there, he'd better do something about his Jewish name.

My uncle understood what he'd been told — the name Morris Roseman is too Jewish for us. But what could he do about his name?

"I'm just Morris," he kept repeating to himself. "Just Morris."

The light bulb clicked on. In short order, he changed his name to Juste Maurice, transforming himself, in the eyes of some, from an unsavory Jewish immigrant to an exotically named musician who might even be delightfully French.

The ploy worked. When Juste Maurice applied again for that job in Boston's schools, he got it and taught music to the city's children for many years before retiring in the early 1970s. Uncle Morris turned anti-Semitism on its head and beat the bigots at their own game.

His career was as colorful as it was varied. Juste performed as a soloist with the Boston Pops at the renowned Jordan Hall, cut 78s with many highly regarded musicians and authored a pair of instructional books: *Foundations of Modern Flute Playing and The Master Introduction for Fife.* You could purchase them together for $1.50.

3. THE DREAM

By the time I reached high school, I was working on a pretty good identity crisis. Deprived of motherly affection at home, bullied by the anti-Semites in school and the neighborhood, certain I was the dumbest kid in town, I had what psychologists today might call serious reservations about my self-worth. I used to ask God, "Why was I born?" There was no immediate answer from On High, so the question continued to torment me.

In one of these bouts of self-doubt, I asked our rabbi, "What's the minimum I need to do to be a good Jew?"

He told me three things, one of which stuck with me to this day.

"Before you can love God," he said, "you have to love his children first."

That was part of the answer, but it was too generic to suit me. How did that relate specifically to me? Why was I born? My family thought they knew:

Hy: "If the name Roseman is ever to mean something, it's up to you."

Ma: "You have two good legs. Your father doesn't. Your brother doesn't. You could dig ditches for a living and be okay."

When I was 8 or 10, I started having The Dream, a recurring nightmare that would invade my sleep regularly for the next 20 years or so. In the dream, I'm standing on the landing of a flight of steps, wondering what I'm supposed to do. My mother is at the bottom of the steps.

"Jump," she says.

Jump? I know I can't make it safely to the bottom in one leap, and that I likely will hurt myself if I try.

"Jump," my mother continues to say.

She's my mother, so she must know what's best for me.

As I jump with blind faith, she moves away. I land on my face at the bottom of the stairs. I know I'm injured, although I don't see any blood. I'm alive but alone as never before.

"Ma, why did you do that?"

"Don't rely on anybody, not even your mother," she says before walking away and leaving me, hurt and defeated, on the floor.

No matter how many times I had this nightmare, it never changed. There was never any variation. My mother says jump, I jump, and she walks away. I was deeply troubled by this dream and so embarrassed by it that I didn't share it with anyone until recently, after it had stopped plaguing me. But back then, I puzzled long and hard over The Dream and its meaning, and I thought I found the answer.

Why was I born? I was born to serve — my family, primarily, but I also would serve any of God's children who needed me. We all were adrift in a single canoe, I imagined; there was only one paddle, I had it, so it was my job to paddle everyone to safety, to prosperity. Jack Roseman didn't exist as a person with his own needs and wants, hopes and fears, except insofar as he was serving others.

And this life of service? I would do it myself, relying on no one, expecting no loving mother to lift me tenderly from the floor and soothe me with kisses. They would see. When I became president of General Motors, I would help them all. The name Roseman would mean something at last.

4. SHORT-ORDER STUDENT

I hadn't thought much about college. With my poor-to-middling transcript and our financial circumstances, college seemed a little lofty, a goal for other people. In my senior year, though, a classmate announced he was attending New York University. After some deliberation, I decided it might be nice to enroll at NYU and go with him. There was still the financial hurdle to overcome. My parents surprised me when they said they had enough money to pay for a semester or two, but whatever it would cover, I was welcome to it.

So I was off to NYU, imagining how wonderful it would be to be out of the cramped apartment, out from under my mother's thumb, out in the rare air. I even picked out my major — chemical engineering, yet another seat-of-the-pants decision.

I hated it. This was my first time away from home, and I hated it. Crazy as it seems, I was so homesick that I hitchhiked from New York to Lynn several times that first semester, just to be back home. It was strange. Tensions may have run high in our apartment, but it was more Cold War than full-battle-gear engagement. At night, I had my hero, my buddy, in bed with me. At NYU I was free, but free to do what? Free to face anti-Semitism by myself? Where do you hide? Where do you go? If you meet somebody new, does he hate Jews generally? This Jew in particular? It was a scary place for me for a while.

All this anxiety crystallized for me one day in chem lab when we were given a liquid and directed to determine its component chemicals, sort of an exercise in reverse engineering. The idea is, when you burn off part of it, you're left with a small amount of liquid that you can analyze. So I went through the burn-off. Then, holding the test tube with the liquid in my left hand, I carefully transferred the residue to a clean test tube in my right hand. Nice job, I thought. But when I looked at the clean test tube, it was empty. No residue.

I checked the floor. There was my precious liquid in a pitiable puddle. When I examined the second test tube more carefully, a found a pin-sized hole in the bottom.

That defective test tube was it for me. I said to myself, the hell with this. I left the lab, left NYU and went home.

I figured I was through with college — I'd already gone through much of my parents' savings. But Hy, who by this time had his master's degree in bacteriology, persuaded me to enroll at the University of Massachusetts, his alma mater. Tuition was reasonable — $100 per semester — and Hy would be nearby to help me through the transition. So I enrolled at UMass and changed my major to math.

Much as I loved Amherst, I still was uneasy away from home. My discomfort wasn't helped by the living arrangements in the dormitory — two to a room, stacked in bunk beds. I didn't mind so much bunking on top, but my roommate was an alcoholic. How he got into college I'll never know. He came in every night well after midnight, falling-down drunk. When he lurched into the lower bunk, it was like an earthquake shaking me awake.

I finally had my fill of it and had a heart-to-heart with him: "Why do you do this? What kind of life are you leading?" I don't know if it was something I said, but he changed somewhat and became more of a human being. It wasn't great, but it wasn't as bad as it was for the first half of the semester.

UMass wasn't the answer, at least at the undergraduate level, so I transferred after a couple years to Boston University. I found my collegiate stride there. BU, of course, is a large, urban university with maybe 30,000 students. Yet those students seemed to be majoring in everything but math. My classes rarely had more than 10 or 15 students, and I loved the personalized attention. It was the warmth I was looking for.

*   *   *   *   *

It was essential for me to work while at BU — once my parents' stash was depleted, I had no money at all — so I applied for a job at Howard Johnson's in Lynnfield, near Boston. Howard Johnson's was an enormously popular chain in the early '50s, and this location was a gold mine. It sat right on U.S. Route 1, a heavily traveled highway to Maine and New Hampshire, so thousands of motorists passed Howard Johnson's every day. In summertime, it wasn't uncommon to see 25 people massed outside the doors waiting for the restaurant to open.

I was hired as a pot washer, absolutely the lowest job in the food chain. My boss was a man named Wilcomb, a decent-but-gruff sort who favored words they didn't teach in the HoJo School of Hospitality.

"Roseman," he said on my first day, "when I walk into the kitchen, all I wanna see are your elbows and asshole."

Not a job to look forward to, but I didn't have to worry about it for long. The restaurant paid its kitchen staff miserably and so experienced near-constant turnover. I was promoted to dishwasher, and it was only a few months later that Wilcomb summoned me from my dishes.

"Roseman, the short-order cook quit. You're the new short-order cook."

I was excited and nauseated at the same time. The pay would be better, but I didn't know the first thing about cooking. On-the-job training wasn't really possible in that busy kitchen. How would I ever handle the rush?

Wilcomb: "Can you scramble an egg?"

Me: "Uh . . ."

Wilcomb: "Can you fry an egg?"

Me: "Well, I . . . "

Wilcomb: "Then you're a short-order cook."

My first day on my new job, a waitress slapped down an order for a Western. I had no idea what that was, so I ran for Wilcomb. I found him stocking the bar. We had another of those conversations that were becoming depressingly familiar.

Me: "Mr. Wilcomb, I don't know what a Western is."

Wilcomb: "Roseman, you are a dumb shit. Take an egg and scramble it — you know how to do that? Put in some chopped ham, a little chopped onion, and fry the damn thing. That's what a Western is."

I hurried back to the kitchen and made the Western. Another waitress hustled it into the dining room and handed me the next order. An Eastern. Back I ran to Wilcomb.

Me: "I got this order for an Eastern."

Wilcomb: "What a dumb fuck you are, Roseman. You know how to make a Western? Leave out the onion. That's an Eastern. Have I ever told you what a dumb fuck you are?"

Thank God we didn't serve Northerns or Southerns!

I worked hard and actually got there most mornings at 6, an hour before my scheduled start time, to help prepare for the rush. I took dozens of eggs from crates and got them cooking so it would take only a few minutes to prepare them as sunny-side up or lightly over. Same thing before lunch. I put a zillion hamburgers on the grill so we would need only a few minutes to prepare them as customers ordered. I even painted the kitchen on my own time. Wilcomb sprang for the paint but wouldn't pay overtime for the work. So there I was, painting the kitchen after my shift ended when I should have been doing my class work.

My industriousness began to attract attention. Several of our part-time kitchen help — they worked full time for GE but actually moonlighted at Hojo despite the low pay — praised my work ethic and told me I would go far. This was music to my ears and an effective antidote to the relentless ear beating I got from Wilcomb.

But even he was impressed and promoted me once more when one of our two chefs was fired. The guy came in drunk but was doing his best to prepare a salmon steak. He spooned on the sauces and seasonings, decorated the plate with lemon and parsley and sent it out to the floor.

We heard a scream from the dining room. The chef had done everything right — except cook the salmon. These days, we could call it sushi and charge double for it. But that wouldn't do in the '50s, so I became the new chef. This time, at least, Wilcomb ordered the other chef to train me.

I must admit that, in all the chaos of the kitchen, I became a pretty good chef, and I really developed rapport with the waitresses. They were tough as nails — had to be to survive in those conditions — but they also were generous, tender, funny, earthy. To this day, I have a soft spot for waitresses and feel a kinship with them. I make a point of chatting with them, asking them about their families, to let them know I appreciate them as people.

However, I found a couple of my new responsibilities disturbing. As might happen in any restaurant, we couldn't perfectly match inventory with demand; inevitably, we had pieces of beef that became old and tough. These should have been discarded, but Wilcomb insisted they be used. You couldn't sell them as such — we'd had enough screaming from the dining room. So I would soften them as best I could, chop them up, lay on spices and use the "aged" beef in stew and meatloaf. You'd be surprised how many compliments I got on those dishes.

Another task was even more disgusting. We had old turkey skins accumulating in the refrigerator. Over time, they molded and should have been totally unusable — or so you would have thought. Wilcomb had another idea: Use them for chicken croquettes. No chicken at all in the croquettes, just the moldy turkey skins.

As an old chicken flicker, I wasn't squeamish about food preparation, but this was too much for me. I invented a number of excuses to get out of it, but eventually, I caved in. How I hated it. I'd need to squeeze a whole lemon over my hands to kill the stench. Yet we never got any complaints from our patrons. (I have every confidence that restaurant food preparation and government inspection of kitchens have improved dramatically since then — at least I hope they have — and that other Howard Johnson's restaurants prepared their food more scrupulously and honestly than ours did.)

One day, we were graced with an important visitor — Mr. Nelson, executive vice president of Howard Johnson's. He ordered fried clams, which I prepared and gave him. He pointed to the floor, where I had unwittingly dropped a clam.

"Those are our profits," he said softly.

But he ordered more clams, then asked for a third order. I thought this was bizarre and realized only later that I was auditioning. Nelson was preparing to open a new Howard Johnson's in the Revere area, about five miles away, and he wanted to see if I could prepare food properly and consistently.

I must have done all right because they offered me the position of trainer in the Revere restaurant and later told me I could be the manager— if I would quit school. This was not a tough choice for me. Managing a Howard Johnson's was a fine position, one many would have killed for. But I didn't think it would take me any closer to the presidency of General Motors. I declined the offer. When I got my degree from BU, my stint as a chef was over.

I was saddened to read recently that by mid-2015, there were only two Howard Johnson's restaurants remaining in America — one in Maine, the other in New York. I think warmly of my time at HoJo. It was a valuable experience that taught me three lessons:

1. If you want to retain and motivate your employees, treat them well and pay them fairly. If you don't, you'll be in constant hiring-training mode, and your business is doomed.

2. If you work hard and show initiative and creativity, management will notice, and they may reward you for your efforts.

3. If you're dining in a restaurant, don't order the chicken croquettes.

* * * * *

I was worn out from working at the restaurant and going to school at the same time. I thought I would test the job market but was advised that no one would hire me because I was still "draft bait." The Korean War was barely in the rear-view mirror, they said, and I was sure to be drafted.

Grad school seemed beyond my reach financially, but Hy rode to my rescue again. He offered to pay my tuition at UMass — he was teaching in the Amherst area and would be able to keep tabs on me. His offer was too good to refuse, but there was one little problem — my transcript. Because I spent so much time at Howard Johnson's rather than studying, my grades suffered. Indeed, when I applied at UMass, I was rejected.

I remembered how Hy had written directly to FDR, and I thought, why can't I do the same? I called the head of the Math Department at UMass, Prof. Anderson.

"I'd like to talk to you about my rejection," I said. "You name the time and place, I'll be there."

When we met, I told him about trying to balance studying and work. I wouldn't be working while in grad school, so I could focus full time on my studies.

"I give you my word," I said. "If you give me a chance to get in, I'll keep up with everybody else. If I don't, ask me once and I'll leave."

He agreed, God bless him, and I was accepted as a grad student.

To save my brother money, I found inexpensive housing — an attic apartment in a home near campus owned by Mrs.

Novack, an old Jewish lady. When I noticed her walking around the house in a long winter coat and gloves, I suspected something wasn't quite right. Sure enough, she kept the thermostat down all year long to save on heating bills. There was no stove in my room to bail me out. I got pneumonia three times in one year.

When Hy came to visit and saw how sick I was, he was furious. He marched to the thermostat, cranked it up to a life-sustaining level and screamed at the landlady:

"I'm putting up this temperature. Don't . . . you . . . move . . . it!"

Superman in the nick of time once more.

*   *   *   *   *

I got my first real taste of romance in college and grad school. When it came to girls, it seemed I was always a bit too young, a bit too shy, a bit too preoccupied. When Lena and her friends went to Revere Beach, I sometimes tagged along. I was just a kid then, but the girls in their bathing suits, the seductive smell of the lotions they used — all that made for a sensual experience for me, though I'm not sure I fully understood that at the time.

Let me tell you how backward I was in this area, how backward we all were. In high school, I once was discussing sex with my two best friends, Jack Servetnick and Jerry Kramer — the son of the resident Communist at the Rosemans' Saturday night roundtable. We were trying to figure out exactly what intercourse involved and where the man was supposed to insert his penis. None of us was sure, though Jerry thought it might be the woman's anus. The City of Sin, my ass. We were in the 10th grade, and this was the state of our collective wisdom. If ever there were a case for sex education in high school, it was the three of us.

Hy tried to help by persuading me to cut school one day and go with him to a burlesque hall in Boston's Scully Square (today called Government Square), which was famous for such establishments. It was the first time I'd seen a naked woman. It was eye opening — as frightening in its way as *The Mummy* — but I was no wiser for the experience.

I remember two girls in the neighborhood — Beverly and Eleanor — that I liked very much, although I was in junior high and still too young to give full expression to my desire. Beverly was what we used to call *zaftig*, full bosomed, which attracted a lot of guys. She wouldn't have anything to do with me. Eleanor, however, my neighbor downstairs on Summer Circle, was a libertine, quite ahead of her time in that regard. She would have been more than willing to initiate me, but I wasn't quite ready.

We did go to the movies once, and it was something of a challenge. The problem: Eleanor wasn't Jewish, and I couldn't let my mother know I had a date with a *schikse*. So we agreed to go to the Waldorf Theatre separately and pretend we met there by chance. *Why, Jack! Fancy meeting you here!* We actually had a lot of fun.

Another time, Eleanor invited some guys to her family's section of our basement and volunteered to show her boobs. (As I say, she was a libertine.) She was about to lift her top when I thought, I can't do this. This is a sin. I ran out of the basement. Hey, I still enjoyed playing marbles. That's where my head was.

Eleanor and Beverly got a kick from my naiveté, and they contrived to tease me. Once when I was alone with them, they lay down, lifted their dresses and showed me their thighs.

"Oh Jaaaa-aaack, which one of us has the better complexion?"

"You're both equal," I said, hightailing it for the door.

In college, of course, I was more sexually aware, and if ever I wanted to read up on romance, Howard Johnson's was like a public library. Everybody was *schtupping* everybody. The waitresses, even the married women among them, were seeing other employees, customers, even deliverymen. These girls were my buddies; I never even considered dating them. (I once was attacked by the brother of a waitress who thought I had insulted his sister. He tripped over my foot as he lunged for me. When he fell, I pinned him, and the fight was over.) Remember, this was the '50s, when people supposedly were raising families in their tidy little homes behind white picket fences, with no thoughts at all of extramarital sex. I laugh every time I see the '50s depicted that way in the movies or on television. I encountered many women in those days and, believe me, they were anything but sexually repressed or unsatisfied.

Several years later, when I was rooming with Jack Servetnick in Cambridge, I did have one semi-serious romance that began in an unusual way. I picked up the phone one day, and a woman on the other end said, "Is Frank there?"

I was in the mood for joking around.

"No, Frank isn't here. Jack is. Can I help you?"

"Maybe you can."

So we got to talking in that flirtatious way.

"Describe yourself."

"Describe *yourself.*"

We fenced like that until I finally asked her to the movies.

She agreed, and our relationship began.

I learned that she wasn't Jewish, that her father was an FBI agent, and that her phone call to me was not a wrong number. She knew perfectly well she was calling Jack Roseman but apparently was leaving herself an out in case she didn't like the sound of my voice or her resolve weakened. What I didn't know was that the downstairs neighbors in the building where she lived were friends of my mother.

Inevitably, Hurricane Bessie found out about our romance and accosted me.

"I just got a call from someone who wanted to know if I knew that my son was seeing her daughter. 'No? Well you ought to know because we're not Jewish.' If you keep seeing this girl, I will have a heart attack."

I had never disagreed with my mother before, much less defied her. But I was an adult now, staking out exciting new territory.

"Ma, I have to see her," I said. "What will be will be."

My new love and I had many good times together, and our romance ended amicably enough. It probably was for the best, for I was about to embark on a passionate affair with a whirlwind.

5. WHIRLWIND II

During World War II, computer technology, driven by the need for real-time military intelligence, had evolved to the point where it presented possibilities for post-war applications; the onset of the Cold War made the need for faster, more capable computers even more urgent. Several institutions were working with the U.S. government on computer development. Among them was Massachusetts Institute of Technology (MIT), not quite in my back yard, but close enough.

The U.S. Navy asked MIT if it could develop a digital computer, rather than a mechanical machine, that could drive flight simulators to train bomber crews. The MIT Servomechanisms Laboratory, under the direction of Dr. Jay Forrester, accepted the challenge. It was a massive project that, between 1948 and its completion in April 1951, employed about 175 people, including roughly 70 engineers and technicians. The budget was a reported $1 million a year, a huge expenditure in those days. When the computer went on-line in 1951, it was dubbed Whirlwind.

Whirlwind was gigantic. It occupied 2,500 square feet and covered fully two floors of MIT's Barta Building. Its vacuum tubes — it used about 5,000 of them — were so large that, if the notion struck you, you could use them to house model ships.

The next iteration was Whirlwind II, which introduced a significant advance — the use of magnetic core memory, which Forrester and his team developed to replace memory that was based on mercury delay lines or cathode ray tubes. This was the great leap forward that enabled Whirlwind II to address the Navy's challenge while laying the foundation for business and personal applications for computers. Harvard University, the University of Pennsylvania and a few other universities also built and housed early computers, but Whirlwind II is the Rose Bowl — the Granddaddy of Them All.

Over time, the Navy lost interest in the project and withdrew. But the U.S. Air Force, aware of the tremendous new capabilities of Whirlwind II, tapped MIT to help construct what would come to be known as the SAGE air defense system, an even more vital objective than the Navy's original mission. The system would feed data about incoming enemy missiles and churn out coordinates that would help the Air Force target and eliminate the would-be infiltrators. In the Cold War, missions didn't get much more important than that.

*　*　*　*　*

Having grown up virtually in the shadow of MIT, I knew it by reputation. But when I got my master's degree, I knew nothing about computers generally, about Whirlwind II specifically, about the Servomechanisms Lab or SAGE. I needed a job, and MIT was one of the places where I applied.

I had toyed with the idea of joining the Air Force. For some reason, I found the prospect of serving as a flight navigator quite appealing; having a master's degree, perhaps I might get that commission. But I discovered that my vision wasn't quite up to Air Force standards, and that, during the McCarthy Era, the only people emerging from grad school with officers' commissions were doctors and clergymen. If I were to begin a military career, it would be as a buck private. Thanks but no thanks. I'd washed enough dishes at Howard Johnson's.

So I combed wants ads in the *New York Times*; I used that

approach more than once in my career. It's fashionable to belittle newspaper want ads, but they've always worked for me — especially in the old days. I sent out more than 50 applications and resumes, got interviews with a handful of companies. MIT was the only prospective employer that called me back for a second interview. That expression of interest on their part sealed the deal for me.

I was hired by Jack Porter, one of the leaders of Whirlwind II, a good man who helped me at several points early in my career. When Jack explained my job to me, I didn't get a real sense of the national magnitude of the project. I got a better feel for that when I was advised that I would need "Top Secret" security clearance to do my job, clearance that was granted with surprising speed and efficiency. Here was the crazy thing about the security that surrounded Whirlwind II: If you were stamped "Top Secret," you could work with the computer, enter data and the like. But unless you had a higher security grade, you couldn't access any of Whirlwind II's output. Even if you were the researcher or scientist who'd entered the data, you couldn't read the ensuing reports without a security upgrade.

My job was to help the Whirlwind II team gauge the accuracy of the U.S. radar system along the East Coast. Accurate radar data would, of course, be critical in the development of an air defense system, so this was a key assignment — and especially challenging for me, since I'd never ever seen a computer before, much less tried to work with a behemoth like Whirlwind II. I had to master computers while simultaneously learning a different type of math involving numerical analysis. And they gave me a deadline for it — nine months.

It was a 24/7 job. Technically, I was living in a Cambridge apartment with my childhood buddy, Jack Servetnick; in reality, I was shacked up in my office, catnapping when I could, all out to meet the deadline. Whirlwind II operated round the clock, every day, so there was no reason why we shouldn't keep that schedule as well. One great benefit of Whirlwind II — it crashed infrequently, a tremendous advance over its predecessors, although it did require considerable maintenance. Thus, there were very few occasions when Whirlwind II was unavailable.

*   *   *   *   *

If ever I needed another reminder of how vital Whirlwind II was to national security, I got one when I received a notice from the draft board in Lynn. I was 25, still draft eligible, and the board advised me that my Uncle Sam wanted me.

I was deeply conflicted. I am nothing if not a patriot. Where else but America would I have the freedom to use my own resources, grand or limited as they might be, to achieve my full potential? Serving my country would have been an honor and, as I say, I'd hoped to join the Air Force. The problem was, Uncle Sam already had me, but I didn't know how much about Whirlwind II I could reveal to the draft board. I explained the situation to my new supervisor, Dr. Frank Verzuh, who had succeeded Jack Porter.

"I'll talk to the board," he said. "You drive me there, wait in the car and don't get involved at all."

So that's what we did, driving from Cambridge to Lynn. I waited in the car while Frank went in to beard the lion. When he returned to the car, he had a funny look on his face.

"One of the board members really has it in for you," he said. "He told me, 'Before I die, I'll see Roseman in the army.' What on earth did you do to that guy?"

I wracked my brain trying to remember how I could have

offended someone I had no recollection of knowing, but I couldn't come up with a thing.

His enmity, it turned out, was of no consequence. As I say, Uncle Sam already had me, and I never heard from the draft board again.

* * * * *

I was able to drive Frank Verzuh to Lynn because, with the income that Whirlwind II was providing, I had purchased my first car, a used 1955 Nash that I absolutely loved. The '55 Nash was so terrific, I figured the '56 model had to be better. So I traded the '55 for the latest model — disaster. I'd had it only a few weeks when, while I was driving, the steering wheel came off in my hands. I don't mean this figuratively. I was holding the steering wheel, which was still attached to the rest of the car by a cable but obviously of no use.

My options for repair were limited as I hardly could drive the car to the dealership — or anywhere else, for that matter. What to do? Then I noticed a series of newspaper ads called "Love Letters to Rambler," testimonials from happy Rambler owners. I remembered how Hy wrote directly to FDR and how I had used the same approach to help reverse the rejection by UMass of my grad school application. Why not try the same strategy here?

I wrote a Love Letter to Rambler, but it was something less than a valentine. It didn't take long to get a response — and it came from George Romney, at that time the chairman and president of American Motors, the same George Romney who would go on to become the governor of Michigan and frequent presidential candidate. He indicated he would send some people around to look at the car. Romney was as good as his word, and I never had another problem with my '56

Nash.

You begin to see something of the Roseman personality here, whether we're talking Abraham, Bessie, Hy or Jack. We draw lines in the sand, and however foolish, proud or quixotic our quests may seem, we don't retreat. We're stubborn.

* * * * *

Another important advance of Whirlwind and Whirlwind II was their ability to, in effect, multitask, something that earlier computers couldn't do. We were able to work on projects other than the air defense system, vital as that was. One of those additional assignments was surprising, and we came to it in an unusual way.

At the time, Princeton's Institute for Advanced Study employed a group of four scientists who were among the tops in their respective fields. When they left Princeton, they seemed a natural fit for Whirlwind II, but their high salaries were an issue. The dean of MIT's Meteorology Department hired the entire quartet — but only by agreeing to pay each of them more than he, himself, was making. That was the scuttlebutt, anyway.

One of the group, a theoretical physicist named Dr. Lewis D. Kaplan, was working on something quite innovative and, to my knowledge, unprecedented: exploring how carbon dioxide emissions trap heat in the atmosphere. The Greenhouse Effect, as it came to be known, was a common enough theme in the '70s, the '80s, and especially in this century, with our concerns about climate change. But this was the mid-1950s, and Kaplan's work was groundbreaking. Even though I was just about flat out on SAGE, when Kaplan asked me for help with his study, I agreed. I found the topic so interesting — possibly important, though I couldn't envision how meaningful the subject would become — that even after I finished my primary Whirlwind II assignment, I continued to work with Kaplan on weekends.

*   *   *   *   *

I met the nine-month deadline, exhausted and unaware how great a toll the work had taken. That became more clear to me when, while visiting my parents, I felt sick and began coughing up blood. The doctor, a kindly man who had survived internment in a Nazi concentration camp, didn't need long to diagnose my condition.

"Bleeding ulcer," he said, "though I've never seen it in someone as young as you. If anybody's going to get ulcers, it's likely to be us Jews. Stress for a Jew is constant."

It wasn't the last time overwork and pressure would lead to a serious health issue. The bleeding ulcer was a clanging alarm, a loud warning that I managed to ignore.

Whirlwind I also was exhausted and already succeeded by Whirlwind II. The rapid development of computers guaranteed that each generation, however innovative at the time, soon would be supplanted by computers even more supple, more capable, more compact. After Whirlwind's work with SAGE was completed, a member of the project team rented it for a reported price of $1 per year. Eventually, some Whirlwind components were housed in the Computer History Museum in Mountain View, California, while a core memory unit went on display at the Charles River Museum of Industry & Innovation in Waltham, Massachusetts.

Not every Whirlwind component made it to a museum. The vast majority of Whirlwind's gigantic vacuum tubes were discarded. On one of my first days working full-time at MIT, I noticed a tube in a trashcan and got permission to take it home. Sixty years later, it still occupies a prized spot atop the bookcase in my home office, a reminder of how far computers have come.

6. FOOTBALL PLAYERS? YOU'RE ALL MATH MAJORS NOW

If you knew computers and math and had even a little experience in those disciplines, it was a great time to be hitting the job market. Whirlwind and Whirlwind II opened the door to business applications for computers, and companies were practically busting that door down, trying to learn how computers could help them.

My old friend Jack Porter, who had hired me at MIT, found one of those early adopters — a large insurance company eager to figure out how computers could give them the edge on their rivals. When Jack asked me for help, I agreed. My assignment was to interview company employees and learn from them what they did. Then, I would determine which functions were best suited for computerization.

A visitor from another planet walking through the company's office would have known right away that this was the 1950s. Dozens of employees, every one a woman, worked cheek by jowl at desks. Amid the desks was the only office with windows; it was for the women's boss, the sole man on the floor.

I had fun interviewing the women, but I realized early on that I had to be careful with my questions. They understood full well that if Jack and I computerized their functions, their employer might no longer have any use for them. Do you remember *Desk Set*, the old Spencer Tracy-Katherine Hepburn movie? Tracy portrays an efficiency expert whom Hepburn fears will render her and her colleagues obsolete. I was Spencer Tracy in this little drama, one that I would see played out dozens of times as the presence of workplace computers grew.

Yet the job wasn't completely fulfilling. I still was working for MIT and Lewis Kaplan on weekends and found my work on campus more satisfying. I'd been toying with the idea of teaching ever since Hy, my role model, chose it as his career. With my experience in math and computers, I thought I could help prepare young men and women for important roles in a dawning industry.

I contacted my old friend, Dean Anderson, at UMass, who was receptive to my coming on board. He hired me as instructor in mathematics. I was back on campus, where I thought I belonged.

*   *   *   *   *

Teaching was a joy. I was so full of myself that I was certain I could reach every student, even in a subject as challenging as math. I had one class that was full of members of the UMass football team. I'm not sure how they all ended up in my class. If they'd heard through the grapevine that this was some creampuff elective where grades were always 'A' or 'B,' they were about to be disabused of that notion. They would have to work to pass my class.

Although I didn't fully appreciate it at the time, I now realize that teaching also satisfied me on another level: Students might hate Jews, but they had to listen to this Jew. Anti-Semitism had knocked me down; teaching elevated me. Was there any basis for perceiving anti-Semitism in my classroom? Definitely not, but you can see the lingering effects of being bullied as a child.

While teaching, I was persuaded by a friend who served on the college's scholarship committee — the group that decided which students would receive aid, and how much — to help out on an informal basis. I was happy to do it, but I soon discovered that so much scholarship money was reserved for football players that the committee actually ran out of cash, unable to help some students it considered deserving.

I was upset, and I'm afraid I took it out on my student-athletes.

"You may be football players," I told them, "but you're all math majors now. I don't care whether you play football or you don't play football. By the time I'm done with you, you will be mathematicians."

It turned out to be one of my best classes. I discovered that athletes respect authority and respond well to discipline. They studied and, for the most part, performed well. In defense of the athletic department, I must add that no one ever told me to take it easy on the football players or alter grades for them.

*　　*　　*　　*　　*

One of the curious aspects of instruction in those early days of computers was that few institutions offered courses in programming. Certainly UMass didn't, but I persuaded Prof. Anderson to allow me to design and teach a seminar-type course in programming.

The results were mixed. My seminar was plagued by bad weather, including heavy snowfalls that made it nearly impossible for off-campus students to make it. One such snowy evening, I found myself greeting only a few students, including a young woman who had braved the elements. There weren't many women pursuing careers in computers back then, so I was curious about her. We chatted for a bit. Her name was Judy Rosenthal, I learned, a sophomore from Boston who loved computers.

I had planned to take the students to see Whirlwind II,

hoping they would find it inspiring. Judy was the only student interested in the excursion, so I gave her a tour of what was, to that point, the world's most important computer. She was duly impressed, and I was impressed that she was impressed. We made arrangements to go out that night. I'm not sure either of us was thinking of a long-term relationship, but on that snowy night, we established a comfort level that made everything else possible.

* * * * *

Much as I loved teaching, I knew I never would be promoted to professor, much less be considered for tenure, without my doctorate. At the same time, Lewis Kaplan suggested that I apply to the Ph.D. program at Brandeis University; if I did, he would provide a strong recommendation. Armed with his support, I applied to Brandeis and was accepted. Brandeis' financial offer was generous: a fellowship, a scholarship and a grant. The total value was around $5,000, almost what I was earning at UMass.

I was seriously pondering the offer when fate intervened in the form of a personnel recruiter from General Electric. I'm not sure how he got my name, but he was charming and persuasive, telling me they really needed someone with both computer and math skills.

"I'm thinking about getting my Ph.D.," I said. "On the other hand, money talks."

"GE's not going bankrupt," he said

He didn't specify what GE would pay me, but I saw dollar signs in my head. I figured I could always get my doctorate, but I wasn't sure if I'd ever again get the chance for the large starting salary that I imagined was in the offing.

"See you Saturday in Schenectady," I said.

The starting salary turned out to be $10,000, double my pay at UMass. Accepting the offer may have been a sound financial move, but I never did pursue my doctorate, a decision I frequently regret. Did the lack of a terminal degree prevent me from doing anything I wanted to do? Probably not, but I'd made a promise to myself and didn't keep it.

*　　*　　*　　*　　*

Although GE had a plant in Lynn, I was posted to GE headquarters in Schenectady. I would be working there as a consultant for GE's operating divisions; I would be available to any GE division or department that needed help with computerization of their operations. It was much like the work Jack Porter and I did for our insurance client, but GE's various units would be my clients, in effect.

I had left home before, but this departure had the feel of finality to it. My father approached me just before I left, his face contorted with feeling.

"I don't know where you're going. I don't know what you do," he said. "But I do know one thing: wherever you go, whatever you do, *sei a mensch*."

His voice was choked with emotion. Be a man of good will, he was telling me, a man of his word. He, too, must have sensed that I would not be back.

I made it to Schenectady by Saturday, but I didn't stay there long. Schenectady was just my mailing address, as I was dispatched to GE plants and offices all around the country. I remember in particular a trip to Irmo, South Carolina, where I was assigned to help a division that made titanium capacitors for the Department of Defense. I was surprised and chagrined to discover that the division general manager held church services for employees each morning.

Attendance was mandatory.

"To get people humble, you have to get them on their knees," he explained. "I get them on their knees."

I was already starting to dislike the corporate culture, although I did hit it off with a GE manager named John Godfrey, a brilliant thinker and inventor who would play a key role later in my career. Another thing that troubled me was the lack of commitment to equality of opportunity. In Irmo, for example, there were plenty of signs posted around the offices pledging equality. But the only black in the Irmo plant was the janitor, a man with a college degree that was getting him nowhere fast.

About one year into my tenure there, GE named a new head for the computer department — the former chief of the light bulb division. What did a light bulb guy know about computers? What hope could I have for promotion if they were picking the light bulb guy to run the computer services unit? This move strongly suggested that the company itself knew little about computers, and that office politics would trump merit where promotions were concerned.

Time to hit the *New York Times* want ads.

7. FAMILY & FAITH: YOU FEEL THE LOVE, AND YOU DON'T QUESTION IT

Judy Rosenthal and her family lived on Beals Street in Brookline, a suburb of Boston about an hour's drive from Lynn. Their home was diagonally across the street from the Kennedy house — yes, *those* Kennedys. Judy never met the Kennedys — they had long since relocated — but John F. Kennedy was born in the upstairs master bedroom of the Beals Street residence and lived there as a toddler. After JFK's presidency and assassination, his mother reacquired the house and, in 1967, donated it to the federal government. The National Park Service today operates the home as a John F. Kennedy National Historic Site.

Judy and I had the right chemistry from the start. Besides being attractive, she was bold and pragmatic at the same time, which meant she could be full of surprises. She was a math major with an interest in computer programming, which pretty well describes my career, to that point. She was Jewish — another plus. We hit it off so well on our tour of Whirlwind II that we began a whirlwind tour of our own.

We went out a few more times and grew even fonder of each other. The only problem with our dating was that I was an instructor at UMass dating a sophomore at UMass. There was no university policy forbidding that — at least, no policy that I was aware of — but I didn't want to set tongues wagging and perhaps embarrass Judy. So I never actually picked her up in her dorm. As luck would have it, her room overlooked the parking lot; when she saw me pull in, she would come to the parking lot and meet me. After each date, we said our goodnights in the parking lot as well.

This all happened in May, just before I moved to

Schenectady to work for GE. In June, I came home each weekend to see Judy. In July, we started talking about a ring. Judy's folks, Fannie and Sam, knew a merchant in the Boston jewelry district, and that's where I bought her ring. When Judy went back to school in the fall, she was a junior . . . and engaged.

We were married Feb. 21, 1960, at the Kehillath Israel Synagogue in Brookline, only a few hundred yards from the Rosenthals' home. The temple had a large, beautiful sanctuary and an adjacent building equally as tall that served as the reception hall. So we had both the service and the reception there. I'm not sure how the invitation list grew so long, but we had over 200 guests. My mother and father were there, as were Lena, Hy, Juste Maurice and Uncle Louis — a rare family reunion for the Rosemans.

We honeymooned in St. Thomas and San Juan, although we spent our first wedded night at the Somerset Hotel in Boston so that we didn't have to rush for a plane right after the wedding. The honeymoon was great, but on the return trip, we encountered problems. We were living in Schenectady, but I had left my car in Boston following the wedding. We landed in New York to find the whole East Coast grounded by a monster snowstorm; all flights were canceled except ours. The airline offered to put us up in a hotel for the night, but every hotel was booked solid.

That left only one possible mode of transportation to Boston: train. We survived a scary taxi ride to the train station and finally made it to Boston. There were no Redcaps at the station because of the storm, so we had to carry our own luggage through the snow. Then, I fell going up the steps of the train and did a job on my shinbone. I couldn't walk right for a month. It was a memorable honeymoon — for many reasons.

We lived on the second floor of a converted one-family home on Cromer Avenue in Schenectady. The house, which was owned by an Italian couple in their 50s, sat on three lots, one of which was a lovely vegetable garden. Our landlady would pick vegetables from the garden, cook them for us and leave the food outside our door. She also made coffee for me on Sunday mornings. They treated us wonderfully, as if we were family.

*   *   *   *   *

Even though excessive work had contributed to, if not downright caused, my bleeding ulcer, even though I was a newlywed with more duties at home than ever before, I didn't modify my work schedule. I'd promised myself that I would make Roseman a well-known name, that I would rise to the presidency of General Motors. How could I achieve those goals except by working 18 hours a day, seven days a week? That's what I did at GE — and for most of my career. That left Judy with an inordinate share of child-rearing and household responsibilities. Unfair as that may seem, Judy understood. We grew up in an era when the husband worked, and the wife was in charge of the household. She did take charge, and she was formidable.

She was, for example, mechanically inclined. If some household appliance broke, she fixed it. If she couldn't fix it, she knew which technicians to call, and she more than held her own in negotiations with plumbers, electricians and other service people. She learned all that, I think, from her father. It was a great stroke of luck for me, because I was — and am — hopeless around the house. My *job* was my job, not fixing toasters. I think another woman would have divorced me, but Judy was a saint. To this day, I call her Saint Jude.

During our "whirlwind" courtship, I learned Judy was smart and practical, with a great sense of humor. I didn't really get to appreciate her determination until we were married. She had promised her parents she would graduate from college, a goal that seemed remote when she left UMass to marry me. But she'd made a promise, and she went to extraordinary lengths to keep it.

When she left UMass, Judy was a few credits short of completing her junior year. Because her grade point average was so outstanding, they allowed her to complete the requirements through home study and, of course, she passed her exams with flying colors. But she still had a year's worth of credits to complete, a difficult assignment for a full-time wife and mother. That we moved every couple years during that period made the task even more daunting. Judy just buckled down and took her courses wherever we landed.

When we lived in Schenectady, she took night classes at Union College because the school didn't allow women in their day program, if you can believe that. When we moved to Virginia, she took courses at the University of Virginia. When we relocated to Maryland, Judy—pregnant with Alan — took the last classes she needed at the University of Maryland. On the day a final exam was scheduled, our little guy decided he wanted to pop into this world two weeks early. Needless to say, Judy missed that exam, but the university allowed her to make it up.

At last, she had her undergraduate degree in math from UMass. She had kept her promise . . . but she wasn't done yet. In the late '70s, when we finally were settled in Pittsburgh, she earned her teaching certificate for secondary math at Duquesne University. Then she learned that the University of Pittsburgh was offering master's degrees in computer science; that was her first love as an undergraduate, but computer science at that time had yet to evolve as a curriculum. Judy applied at Pitt, which accepted her on condition that she take three undergraduate courses in computer science to fill in what she'd missed. She did that and earned her master's degree in the early '80s. It had taken five institutions and two decades, but Judy persevered and got the education and degrees she wanted. Plus, when I suffered serious health problems that began in the 1970s, Judy knew that she was highly employable and could support our family if necessary.

At Union College, we actually took a night course together — Numerical Analysis was the course name. Judy earned a better grade than I did. I assured her that, because of my greater experience in the field, I was reading too much into what the instructor asked on the final exam and provided answers that were far over his head. But she didn't beat me up with her superior grade. Fact of the matter is, with her brains and determination, had she opted for a full-time career in math or computer science, she might have run rings around her husband. Don't you dare tell her I said that.

* * * * *

Judy's parents, Fannie and Sam Rosenthal, were terrific in-laws, terrific people. There was nothing they wouldn't do for us, whether it was babysitting the kids or buying us things for the house. Yet there were issues between us. If anything, they were *too* generous. Remember, I was going to make it on my own, relying on no one, not even family. That was the meaning of my recurring dream. So each time they presented us with a gift for the house, it embarrassed and angered me, as if they were leading me to betray my dream.

From their point of view, I had spirited away their only daughter. And since Judy's brother Bob was eight years her senior, she was more like an only child to Fannie and Sam. And here I was, a member of the faculty at UMass, a guy with a bleeding ulcer no less, seducing their impressionable daughter — only a sophomore at that. I didn't understand where they were coming from. Today, I certainly do. Had our positions been reversed, had some faculty member — with or without a bleeding ulcer — wanted to marry my innocent young daughter, I'm sure I would have opposed it. It took me many years to understand this. At the time, though, I sometimes felt like an outsider around them.

Sam was a smart guy, an accountant with a degree from Northeastern University in Boston. More importantly, the term "people person" might have been coined with Sam in mind. Once, when he was preparing to paint the Rosenthal house in Brookline, he selected three or four colors of paint that he liked and brushed a sample of each on a sort of palette. Then he went knocking on doors, showing the palette to his neighbors across the street and asking them which color they preferred.

"We all spend a lot of time on our porches," he told them, "so you'll see my house a lot more than I will. Pick the color you like."

That sort of thing earned him the affection and respect of everyone.

I found one chink in Sam's armor of generosity. Being so proud and independent, I insisted that whenever Judy and I went out with her parents, we would split expenses. So if we went to dinner, Sam would buy one time, I would buy the next time. After a while, I noticed that when it was Sam's turn to buy, he'd order a hamburger or some other inexpensive item. When it was my turn to buy, he somehow had a taste for the best, priciest steak on the menu. I really got a charge out of it; I appreciated that, in his way, Sam was teaching me a lesson.

We finally broke the ice between us on the occasion of the Rosenthals' 35th wedding anniversary, when Fannie and Sam invited Bob and his wife and Judy and me to dinner at the Somerset Hotel. Sam even ordered a limo for all of us to make it an elegant affair — and to allow us to drink at dinner without having to worry about driving afterwards. We were having cocktails before dinner, chatting about this and that, when Sam grabbed my hand and said, "Jack, you are a sonofabitch." I heard in his voice a mix of admiration and affection, and it changed our relationship. After that, I felt completely at ease with Sam. We both smoked cigars in those days — Cubans (when I could get them) for me, El Productos for Sam. We wiled away more than a few hours puffing and laughing and even talked about going into business together.

Alas, Sam died at 62, just four years after Judy and I were married and not too long after that memorable 35th anniversary wedding celebration. The cemetery where we buried him is about an hour's drive from Boston, yet the number of friends who came to pay tribute to Sam was unbelievable. If you looked back up the highway from the cemetery, you couldn't see the end of the line of cars.

When Judy and I visit the cemetery, I always leave an El Producto on Sam's grave to show my respect for him. I don't believe in an afterlife, but hey, just in case.

*   *   *   *   *

We both wanted children, although I think I may have been a little more gung-ho than Judy was. I told her I wanted a dozen kids; I may have been joking but with some element of truth. Then reality sets in. You start out wanting 12 kids.

When you have one, you decide, well maybe we'll have five. Then when you have two, you say, maybe four. After Alan, our second child, was born, there was no question we would go for three and stop there. But if Judy had wanted two or three more after that, she wouldn't have heard a peep from me. I used to tease her — have as many kids as you want so long as they're at least 2 years old. I can relate to them better.

Our three children are wonderful — and wonderfully different. Their one common trait was shyness in varying degrees. We learned over time not to push them to be more outgoing because telling a shy person she's shy just makes her even more shy. So we let them blossom at their own pace. Another thing they had in common — piano lessons. Judy insisted that they have music in their lives, and she believed strongly that knowledge of the piano provided the best foundation for any other instruments they might try. So they all experienced three years of piano lessons, willingly or not.

Let me introduce our kids to you.

Laura Lee Roseman Kalchthaler

Laura was born in Schenectady in 1961, just a few days after Judy and I celebrated our first wedding anniversary. About a year later, when I signed on with CEIR, we moved to Bailey's Crossroads in Virginia. In Schenectady, we lived in what used to be a single-family house that the owners converted into two units. We had a tiny kitchen, a bedroom, a living room and more or less a closet off the living room. There was a little entry hall on the first floor from which you either walked through a door into the landlords' unit, or you walked up the stairs to ours. We used to keep Laura's carriage in the hall. If we wanted to go out at night, we'd push the carriage into the landlords' apartment, and they would take care of our baby. When we got home, we would just open their door and pull the carriage back out. It was a nice situation, and we grew to love that house and our landlords. We had it all — apartment, utilities, fresh-cooked food, babysitting — for $19 per week.

All our kids were good babies, Laura especially so. As she grew, she developed into an unusually mature young lady, although I'm not sure she always enjoyed the responsibility of being the eldest. No matter where she might have been — a friend's house, overnight camp — she would not go to bed until her room looked like she had never been away, everything in its place.

Laura wanted to be a nurse until a friend suggested that she become a dental hygienist instead. The hours are better, there are no bedpans to empty, and probably no one would die on your watch. That sounded good to Laura. She enrolled at the Forsyth School for Dental Hygienists, an affiliate of Northeastern University, her Grandpa Sam's alma mater. Being in Boston, Laura was near both the Roseman and Rosenthal families, which eased the difficulties of being so far from home, and she became particularly close to Fannie, Judy's mother. She returned to Pittsburgh with a Dental Hygiene license and began working three days a week in Pittsburgh.

At the same time, Laura pursued a degree in management information systems from LaRoche College, which is a stone's throw from our home in Pittsburgh's North Hills suburbs, switched to accounting and got her bachelor's degree in that field, cum laude. While raising her children, she worked two jobs – dental hygienist and owner of her in-home stationery business, The Write Touch. When her children were older, she worked two part-time jobs – dental hygienist and operations specialist for a local Raymond James branch.

Finding the love of working for a large corporation, Laura switched to full time employment with Raymond James. An additional perk is the tuition reimbursement, as Laura is pursuing her MBA through California University of Pennsylvania.

Laura and her ex-husband, Earl Kalchthaler, have three wonderful kids — Sheena, Kyle and Faylyn — who are about ready to embark on their careers, and they couldn't find better professional models than their parents. Earl served as a Navy MP in Vietnam as the war was winding down. He comes from a long line of butchers and began his career in that field but decided he wanted to try something different.

He earned his associate's degree at Community College of Allegheny County and began studying for a degree in criminal justice at Pitt while he was working as a supermarket butcher. One of the requirements was a course in computer science — funny how computer science always pops up in the Roseman family. Judy was his mentor for that course, often spending Saturday nights with Earl at Pitt's computer lab. After earning his degree, he landed with a company called Renewal, a halfway house for prisoners. Through a series of promotions, he's now in charge of the federal prisoners at Renewal — quite a responsible position that keeps him on call round the clock.   *   *   *   *   *

Alan Steven Roseman

Our son was born in 1963 when Laura was 2, prompting our move to a bigger house in Silver Spring. The house was fine; Alan wasn't. He had hearing problems that impeded his ability to speak. When you talked to him, he heard your voice as if it were muffled or coming through a primitive telephone system with lots of static. He was 3 when doctors removed his tonsils and adenoids — a common enough procedure that we thought would remedy his problems immediately. Now, however, he was like a newborn, hearing sounds for the first time and struggling to repeat them.

We enrolled him at a special Easter Seals program — five days each week for two years. They did wonders with Alan, but he still started kindergarten a year late and needed speech therapy until he started high school. How ironic that communication problems kept Alan from starting school on schedule — just as they did his father. Different type of problem, to be sure, but the impact was the same.

At Easter Seals, he was the most polite, best-behaved student there. His teacher considered Alan a little too quiet for his own good.

"I would be the happiest person in the world if I ever had to discipline your son," the teacher once said to me. "He's perfect. He doesn't do anything to disrupt the class."

She actually called me at work one time to report a breakthrough — she'd had to discipline Alan. I jumped for joy. Sounds crazy, I know, but we considered that a big step on the path to a healthy childhood.

When Alan was a pre-teen, I encouraged him to take up a hobby that we could share. Sports were pretty much out of the question, since I was one of the few American males to have grown up without throwing a baseball, kicking a football, dribbling a basketball or hitting a golf ball. The hobby he chose: collecting beer cans. This isn't as odd as it seems, since beer can collecting was a popular pastime then. As usual, I didn't jump in halfway. Alan and I not only saved beer cans, but I became a dealer as well. On many Sundays, I drove the few miles to the Wildwood Flea Market, set up a table and bought and sold beer cans. I had cans that sold as cheaply as 50 cents and a few that were quite valuable as collectibles. The crown jewel was a can of Cape Cod Ale. At that time, there were only six of those babies in the entire U.S. — six that had been verified, anyway — and I paid $900 for it. Eventually, Alan got tired of our hobby, but I kept at it — with Judy's help — for several decades.

After Alan's obligatory three years of piano (The Judy Rule), he played the drums and excelled at it. When he was a senior in high school, his class performed Christmas music at an assembly, and Alan played a featured role — the Little Drummer Boy. That probably was the highlight of his musical career. He became great friends with Ron Abbott, the drum major. They enrolled at Indiana University of Pennsylvania and roomed together all four years. Ron and Alan, who wasn't playing drums anymore, became cheerleaders. Their relationship was very interesting. Ron was completely responsible for Alan's social life. Alan was responsible for seeing that Ron graduated. They were in each other's wedding and have stayed close over the years.

Alan earned his degree in management information systems at IUP and continued on for his MBA at Pitt. He was ready for the job market, but his timing was terrible. It was only a few weeks after he graduated from Pitt that the American economy was rocked by Black Monday — Oct. 19, 1987. The crash created havoc in the stock market and business world. Alan tried mightily to get a job, leaving the house early in the morning to knock on doors, coming home in the evening with only another frustrating day to show for his efforts.

Eventually, he encountered a small Pittsburgh company for sale and applied for a bank loan to finance the transaction. The same day he was approved for the loan, he opened the mail to find a job offer from a Florida company that sold security equipment for businesses. Now, he had a decision to make. Buy the Pittsburgh business or accept the Florida job? Judy and I suggested that he take the job. Our sense was that he could buy a company anytime, but the job was an opportunity to learn real-world business on somebody else's dime. He stayed with that company about a year before moving to one of their rivals, a business called Sensormatic, which also is based in Florida.

It turned out to be the key move of his career. He rose spectacularly at Sensormatic, earning a series of promotions. He even served a stint in sales to get a better feel for what the reps were experiencing in the field. Among his most important customers were casinos, which need security for two reasons: to make sure patrons aren't robbed and to make sure the state gets every penny to which it's entitled.

When he was in sales, Alan once took me with him to one of his customers, a casino outside Hartford called Foxwoods that's owned by the Mashantucket Pequot Tribe. At one time, it was considered the largest casino in the world in terms of gambling space and number of slot machines. The top floor of the hotel was reserved for high rollers, who got as much food and booze as they wanted, courtesy of Foxwoods. Through Alan's connections, I got to spend some time on the high-roller floor, where I was introduced to a member of the tribal council. He explained to me that all members of the tribe received free houses and education.

I was struck by his bright red hair.

"Pardon me for saying it, but you don't look Native American."

"I'm one-eighth Native American."

"One-eighth and you're on the council?"

"There are very few purebreds here, very few. My grandmother was purebred."

I thought, if a one-eighth Native American can get free housing and education, a purebred Ukrainian-American-Jew ought to get something. Foxwoods was a great experience with some fun people.

After a number of years with Sensormatic (which was purchased by Tyco), Alan shifted over to a company called Intelligent Marketing, which serves as a manufacturer's representative for Sensormatic and other lines of security equipment. He has a huge territory covering the entire Eastern Seaboard of the United States from Maine to Florida.

Alan and his wife, Tina, now live in Exton, near Philadelphia. Tina is a terrific tennis player, cook and entertainer. Their daughters, Paige and Brooke, have their parents' talent and drive. I have no doubt they'll make their mark.

* * * * *

Shari Beth Roseman Waldman

With her outstanding grades, Shari was accepted at both Carnegie Mellon University and Allegheny College in Meadville, PA. Everyone was thrilled by her plans to enroll at CMU, and we wasted no time sending them the $300 deposit. Turned out there was a hitch. In May of Shari's senior year in high school, CMU notified her that, because she was a local student, she would have to live at home until they figured out how many students actually matriculated, a process that could take four or five weeks. Shari didn't want to miss orientation or those first few weeks, so she enrolled at Allegheny instead. I wrote a letter to CMU demanding the return of our deposit; they complied. Shari was crestfallen with this turn of events, yet I think it worked out well for her.

At Allegheny, she discovered she was one of only 10 students majoring in computer science, assuring that all 10 would get maximum attention. The faculty and culture there were fantastic. Students didn't learn computer science only — they learned how to learn. Students were responsible for the material in the textbooks, but in class, the professors were innovative and challenging. At other schools, if you take good notes, you can pass the tests. Not at Allegheny. Each undergraduate even had to write a thesis, something you'd expect in a master's degree program, to graduate.

Shari pursued her master's in computer science at the University of Maryland. Upon graduation, she went to work for an aerospace company that was sold several times and now is part of Lockheed Martin in Gaithersburg, MD. Incredible as it may seem, she worked on the same federal aviation project, sitting at the same desk, using the same telephone number, for many years. She tired of it once and signed on with a local consulting company. But she found she missed her professional "family," and Lockheed Martin welcomed her back after about a year. She returned to the same desk, same telephone number. When she retrieved her voicemail, she found the same messages that were there when she left.

Shari's courtship with her future husband, Carl Waldman, a neurologist from Pittsburgh who was working in northern Virginia, was right out of a Hollywood romance. Shari and two friends had signed up for a cruise, paying a little extra for the third person in the room. Carl had signed up as a single, paying a little extra for the privilege of his own room. About five months before the trip, the cruise line staged a happy hour get-together for passengers. Shari and Carl met there and found they had much in common. Each was single, about 40 and with ties to Pittsburgh.

You can guess the rest. For the next five months, Shari and Carl dated. By the time the cruise rolled around, the threesome had become a twosome, and Carl's single room had another occupant.

Shari and Carl — and their rescue dog, Peanut — currently live in the same townhouse Carl bought when he first started working. That gives them considerable flexibility to pursue any professional opportunities that arise.

*   *   *   *   *

Having a wife and family changed me enormously. Yes, I still worked ridiculously long hours and didn't spend enough time with the kids, but my outlook on life changed dramatically. Back when I was single and traveling for GE, I sometimes flew Eastern Airlines on a turboprop plane called the Electra, which had some problems. Every so often, an Electra would plunge from the sky, wiping out everybody aboard. In those days, I never worried about boarding a potential death trap. I would observe my fellow passengers and think: "How can you get on this plane? So many people are depending on you. But if the plane crashes and I die, no one's life will miss a beat."

Once I married, once Laura was born, my thoughts on boarding a plane were quite different. Now, I was as miserable and apprehensive as everyone else was. Flying became a matter of faith for me, and faith was a big issue I had to consider for my family.

What role should Judaism play in the lives of my children, in the life of my family? I was raised a Conservative Jew, of course, and yet, I'm by profession and inclination a mathematician. What we know in mathematics is that you can prove just about anything you want, depending on your assumptions. If you like, you can prove that God exists. If you're so disposed, you can prove that he doesn't. For that reason, I'm neither religious nor an atheist.

But Judy and I wanted our kids to know what it means to be Jewish — not so much the laws and holy books as the Jewish identity and culture. If anything, Judy felt even more strongly about this than I. She never went to Sunday school or *cheder*, but as a teenager, she joined Young Judaea and went to Tel Yehudah, their summer camp in New York. She wanted our children to have similar experiences. *What does it mean to be Jewish?* We wanted our kids to ask that question . . . and discover the answer.

This focus on faith became especially important for us when I joined On-Line Systems and we moved to Pittsburgh in 1970. We bought a house in Pittsburgh's North Hills suburbs, a young, growing area where Jews were few and far between. In fact, if I remember correctly, we were something like the 27th family to join Temple Ohav Shalom — called North Hills Jewish Community Center at the time — which was always on the lookout for Jewish families new to the North Hills. We actually had a member named Phyllis Rosenfeld who would call people recently relocated to the northern suburbs.

"Your name sounds Jewish," she would say. "Are you?"

Judaism never had a saleswoman like Phyllis.

There were so few Jewish families in the community that the temple could not yet afford to construct a building. Every other Friday night, a different family would host *Shabbos* services in its game room. We may not have had a proper temple, but we did have a Torah, a portable Torah that my friend Ted Barnett lovingly transported in the back of his station wagon. Wherever the services were that Friday, it was Have Torah-Will Travel.

The Roseman kids often were the only Jews in their classes, which created some challenges. Laura became good friends with a girl named Vickie, a born-again Christian, although we didn't call them that in those days. Laura came home from school one day, very upset because Vickie told her people like Laura couldn't go to heaven because they didn't believe in Jesus. Judy was able to calm Laura, assuring her that Vickie was acting out of love rather than hate. That was the atmosphere in the North Hills, but we persevered. All our kids went to Sunday school and Hebrew school. Alan was bar mitzvah'd, and Laura and Shari were bat mitzvah'd.

*   *   *   *   *

A few years ago, when our eldest grandchild, Sheena, was visiting us, she clearly had something on her mind.

"Sometimes I believe you're religious," she said to me, "and sometimes I don't. Who is your God? Describe him."

I took Sheena downstairs to the porch and pointed up at the eaves.

"Every spring, the robins make nests there. These birds, with their tiny little brains, make nests better than you or I ever could. Whoever taught the robins to make their nests that way, that's my God. You can call him Allah, Jesus, Adonai. You can call God evolution. God is the miracle of life. That's what I believe."

Sheena shook her head.

"Then why do you call yourself a Jew?"

"If all men were equal and there were no prejudice in the world, I would call myself a human being, nothing more and nothing less. But as long as there's a disadvantage to being Jewish, as long as Jews are rounded up and sent to concentration camps, as long as Jews are discriminated against, then I'm a Jew. If Jews are made to suffer, then this Jew will suffer."

I don't think Sheena completely grasped my explanation. That's sometimes the way it is with family and faith. You feel the love, and you don't question it. You embrace it.

8. "NBC PROJECTS THE WINNER WILL BE..."

When I left GE, computer services was still a hot sector, and few companies were any hotter than CEIR. It was founded as a nonprofit called Council for Economic and Industry Research, a vague title that didn't begin to suggest the high-level nature of its work. An employee named Dr. Herbert William "Robby" Robinson — he had doctorates in both economics and statistics from the London School of Economics and Oxford University — bought the company, renamed it CEIR and took it public. Although Robinson bought the business for a bargain-basement price — we heard it was $25,000 — it became a stock market darling and expanded significantly, with offices in New York, Los Angeles, San Francisco, Houston, Chicago, Atlanta, Boston and Washington, DC.

Robinson once invited a group of his employees, including me, to the estate he'd purchased in Virginia. From the window of his home, the view was lush, green grass as far as the eye could see. I couldn't help but comment.

"Robby, you've done well."

"Why shouldn't I do well?" he said. "I have two doctorates."

Okay, a little snobbery there, but you have to admire him for his vision to purchase CEIR for so little and transform it to a high-flier.

Government work, often at the Top Secret level, was CEIR's mainstay. The company counted NASA and the Department of Defense among its regular clients. One of its most important federal contracts was to monitor the goods and services imported to, and exported from, the Soviet Union. Economists call this "input/output analysis." This was considered a critical mission during the height of Cold War tension, one that entitled CEIR to special treatment.

For its work on that contract, CEIR for many years did not send invoices, never had to wait 30 or 60 days for payment. Each Friday, a CEIR employee would show up at the offices of the United States Treasury. Each Friday, Treasury would cut him a check. This was an extraordinary arrangement that showed just how important the government considered CEIR.

CEIR hired me as head of the mathematics group under Jack Moshman in its Washington office. This was not quite so innocuous as it sounds, as I led a team of perhaps 50 people — mathematicians, programmers, statisticians, economists — with an impressive variety of advanced degrees. We were a one-stop shop for clients, developing computer models to organize, access and manipulate data, even compiling the data if the client lacked that capability. It was a great team; the Washington office soon was CEIR's leading producer.

*   *   *   *   *

Government work may have been our bread and butter, but it was another assignment that probably was of more lasting significance. In the early 1960s, NBC came up with the concept of using computers to help Huntley and Brinkley — the most famous news duo of the day — project winners in all the high-profile national elections, including the U.S. presidency.

The idea was that my team would gather, organize and input data from key precincts according to a model that we would develop. Based on that information, our computer would spit out a projection, which would be delivered to Huntley and Brinkley while they were live on the set. Our computer would be hidden behind a curtain on the set.

Nowadays, of course, we're used to seeing reporters and analysts touch a "magic screen" to produce current and historical election data. Back then, this was a pioneering effort, and all that information had to be assembled through laborious research.

When we sat down to negotiate the contract with NBC, they wanted a penalty provision, whereby CEIR would return a portion or all of our fee if we failed to deliver data in a timely fashion.

"If you're even a day late, people will have read the results in the newspaper," NBC said. "We have no use for it. So what should be the penalty if you're late?"

This ignited a heated discussion, and I have to give Moshman credit. He didn't give even an inch. In the end, we signed a contract that did not include a lateness penalty; no one could come up with a penalty that would make up for tardy data.

I learned a little about television — probably more than I wanted to know. My sense was that we would print out projections, run them to Huntley-Brinkley, and that would be that. Live TV, as I soon discovered, doesn't work that way. The director made us rehearse the entire process. He would time us with a stopwatch. If we were even a second or two off — the runner got the slip to the news desk two seconds late, say — he would have a fit, and we'd have to perform yet another dry run.

While our contract with NBC had no lateness penalty, it did feature one unusual provision. Moshman and I, as well as most other members of our team, had to agree not to travel on the same flight when we were shunting between CEIR in Washington and NBC in Cherry Hill, New Jersey, lest we all be wiped out and take NBC's project with us. I paid little attention to this provision, defied it on several occasions, so you probably can guess what happened next.

Most of the team was on a plane headed from Washington to Cherry Hill to finalize the de-bugging of the computer programs we'd created for NBC. One of my guys, a relentlessly small-picture statistician named Dorfman, buttonholed me on the plane about improvements he wanted to make on the statistical side.

"I just thought of a new model that would be a little better than the old model," he said. "Can we change it?"

"Wouldn't be wise at the moment."

Dorfman spun his pitch a little to try to make it more appealing to me. All of a sudden, we noticed that more than Dorfman was spinning; the plane was pitching and yawing. Our little group was having trouble sitting, let alone standing. The plane tried to descend for a landing but bounced right back into the sky — landing gear malfunction. A flight attendant tried to reassure us.

"Don't worry, everything will be fine," she said, but she sobbed as she said it.

Passengers were dealing with their impending demise in different ways. The woman behind me had slipped into a state of semi-shock.

"First time I've ever flown," she mumbled repeatedly. "Last time I'll ever fly."

Dorfman, though, was oblivious to it all.

"If we do it this new way, I'm sure the model will be better, and there's not much reprogramming involved."

I was certain we were going to die, and I didn't want Dorfman's whining to be my last thoughts.

"Whatever you want, you'll get. Just sit down and kindly be quiet."

Eventually, we descended once more and hit ground, *sans* landing gear. Protective foam covered the runway, which was lined with emergency vehicles. When we finally skidded to a stop, we were ordered to deplane on a slide that, if you're lucky, you'll see only in movies.

Dorfman still was in the Dorfman Zone, nattering on about the model.

"Fuck you," I said. "You ain't getting any changes."

"But you said — "

"What I said I said because I thought we were about to die. Now that we're still alive, you ain't getting any changes."

The adventure wasn't quite over. A bus picked us up after we slid from the plane. As we boarded, I could hear someone muttering over and over: "First time I've ever flown. Last time I'll ever fly."

When we arrived at NBC, everyone in the office was agog about the plane that had crash-landed. Fortunately, no one on our team said something stupid like, "I know. We were on it." That would have been an acknowledgement of our clear violation of the contract. So we played dumb.

"A plane crash-landed? Really?"

Everything worked out well. Huntley-Brinkley was able to use our data to forecast the election winners of 1964. (This was not without controversy, as the network made its calls more than four hours before the polls on the West Coast closed.) The head of the project for NBC moved along to ABC, which hired us to handle projections for the next election cycle.

I read an obituary of Robby Robinson — he died in 2013 — that indicated CEIR was the first to provide data for election forecasts. That certainly is not the case. In 1952, CBS asked Remington Rand to provide election projections using UNIVAC, considered the first commercial computer produced in America. UNIVAC became an icon for this new phenomenon known as computers, viewed as comical and threatening at the same time. But the approach to election forecasting in those early years tended to be one dimensional and dangerous, with projections based entirely on early returns and key precincts. If those initial returns were from precincts heavily skewed to one party or the other, projections could have been dead wrong. As it turned out, UNIVAC got it right. In fact, the data showed Eisenhower routing Stevenson by such a wide margin that the computer operators at first didn't pass along the numbers, not trusting their own work.

Concepts such as exit interviews would come along later. CEIR wasn't the first in this business, but I like to think we advanced the state of the art.

*   *   *   *   *

This was my first real supervisory position, and it forced me to develop a managerial style. Among the elements in that style was community involvement. Without ever consulting me about it, Jack Moshman got me involved in two important trade organizations: the D.C. chapter of the Association for Computing Machinery (ACM) with about 7,000 members, primarily programmers, and the American Federation of Information Processing Societies (AFIPS), which was an umbrella organization for a number of groups, including ACM, the American Institute of Electrical Engineers and the Institute of Radio Engineers. The more I thought about it, the more I realized what a good idea community involvement is. I was devoting 100 percent of my effort to making money for CEIR, but what was I contributing to society? These organizations were a way to give back, and I resolved to allocate at least 5 percent of my time — 10 percent if I could manage it — to the community.

I had no trouble reaching and exceeding that goal because I took on the role of program chairman for the 1964 AFIPS conference, which was *the* industry gathering in the United States. I also served as chairman of ACM's DC chapter, an even tougher task requiring the organization of a meeting in Washington every month.

Lining up speakers for ACM meetings involved a lot of legwork, but I was able to bring in industry leaders and policymakers, including U.S. Sen. Hubert Humphrey. The tougher part of the job was standing up before hundreds of people each month and speaking to them. I couldn't avoid addressing them — I was the chairman, after all — but the prospect terrified me. Here was little Yonkil Roseman, held out of school for a year because he couldn't speak English, having to stammer along before his peers. I hated the thought of it, hated myself even more for fearing it. I girded myself and got through it. With each passing month, public speaking became more routine to me. I won't say I excel at it, but at least the mere thought of it doesn't make my palms sweat.

As often happens, these public service efforts came back to me many times over. Working with ACM and AFIPS, I got to know a lot of people, including government managers who controlled various budgets. It became quite common for me to call them and ask if there were some way they could help me meet my monthly sales quota. Jack, they would say, come over and we'll talk.

Yet another component of my emerging style was bringing employees into the decision-making loop as much as possible. I began to hold one-on-ones with staff — impromptu sessions right in their offices.

"What went wrong?" I would say.

Typically, the employee would give me the party line.

"That's a good reason. Now tell me the *real* reason."

This was an invitation to drill down into the workings of the company. Often, we would jointly identify processes that we could correct, which was a terrific outcome. Even if we didn't unearth anything concrete, the employees learned that I valued their opinions and was receptive to their input.

I showed my respect and concern for employees in yet another way — allowing them to come and go as they pleased. In my department, we had no specific starting or quitting times. This made nothing but sense to me for a number of reasons. First, our jobs were demanding — our computers were available 24/7 — and many of our employees were trying to balance work and family life. Giving them time to spend with their families was the humane thing to do, and it endeared CEIR to them. Just as importantly, our staff included a lot of creative genius types who would throw themselves into a project and work until they were in danger of burning out. A flexible schedule allowed them time to relax and recharge their batteries. I became a devotee of flexible scheduling and carried it with me throughout my career. I follow a flexible schedule myself, so why shouldn't others have the same benefit?

Another cause that I came to champion was long-term disability insurance for employees. I learned the value of this protection when one of our people suffered a cerebral hemorrhage. Even though the repercussions were severe, he returned to work because he had little choice — CEIR didn't offer long-term disability insurance. Under those circumstances, I wouldn't have felt right dismissing him. My department was doing very well, so I figured we could carry him. I expected no production from him and got exactly that. This experience taught me one thing: as long as I have any say in the matter, our company will offer long-term disability insurance because I remember what that guy went through . . . and what I went through worrying about him.

It was a maverick style I was developing, so it was no surprise that it got me in deep trouble with senior management.

* * * * *

Personnel changes are common in corporations, even more so in a growing, uncharted field such as computer services was at that time. But CEIR hit me with a big one when they kicked Jack Moshman upstairs to the corporate level and replaced him with Claggett Jones. I discovered quickly that my new boss was a strong proponent of the conventional wisdom.

One day, Jones got to the office about 8:30 and noticed no more than a handful of people there. I typically rolled in about 9:00. When I did, Jones was waiting for me. His greeting was not in the warmest Welcome Wagon tradition.

"We start at 8:30 here, Jack, and we leave at 5. I expect you to enforce those hours."

"From the reports I've seen," I said, "we're the most profitable of the company's offices. You know why? We give people the opportunity to be their best. The place is open 24 hours a day because the computers are running 24 hours a day. If you come in at midnight, at 3 in the morning, you'll see people here. I don't want to change that. You start making them work 8:30 to 5, you won't get the productivity."

Because I was insistent on this, Jones let that pass. But he imposed a rule that all CEIR projects must have 10 milestones, a preposterous example of management by textbook to which I objected.

"You're telling me a $10,000 contract and a $1 million contract each should have 10 milestones?"

"Yes."

"Why not 15?"

"Because I didn't think of 15. I thought of 10."

I thought, geez, I'm arguing with a nut and left it at that. But you don't talk to your boss this way without repercussions. Soon, I had Jones' answer.

He introduced me to Edgar Eichorn, a Ph.D. who had worked under the famous chemist/biochemist Dr. Linus Pauling. Eichorn, Jones said, was my new supervisor and would occupy my office—my spacious, airy office. I would be relocated to a tiny, cramped closet that was masquerading as an office.

"If I had my way, you'd be out of this company," Jones said. "But Edgar convinced me that you should stay."

Eichorn wanted to meet his key people (until that moment *my* key people), so I introduced him to Eli Hellerman, a linear-programming whiz who had a national reputation as one of the best in his field. Eichorn noticed a picture on the wall above Eli's desk. His mouth turned sour.

"I see that you don't have a frame on that picture. A picture worth hanging is worth framing."

Eli stared at him incredulously.

"Let me put it this way: if I come in this office next week, that picture better be down or it better be framed."

This was not the way you dealt with people like Eli. He quit, and he was followed out the door by some of the best employees we had.

To add insult to injury, Eichorn conducted my performance review and concluded that I was being overpaid — by $500 per year.

"Edgar," I said, "why don't we leave it this way. If I don't see a 10 percent increase in my salary at the end of this month, I'll assume you're telling me to leave."

"You're bluffing," he said.

"We'll know at the end of the month."

At the end of the month, my salary was up 10 percent. It may have seemed like they were trying to make conditions so miserable for me that I would leave voluntarily, but I don't think that was the case. Most of the competent employees already had abandoned them. I was one of the few left.

I may have won that little battle, but the war was getting to me. I asked Judy if she thought I should resign. Her answer, wise as always, helped restore my perspective.

"If you think people respected you only because of your title and big office, then you should leave. If they respect you because they like you and know your capabilities and what you've done for the company, you have no reason to leave."

We came up with a plan: I would stay at CEIR until I got promoted. But the day I got that promotion, I would quit.

Less than a year later, the corporate wheels turned once more. Moshman was back. Jones and Eichorn were out.

Moshman offered to put me in charge of professional services for the East Coast, spanning CEIR's offices in Boston, New York and DC.

"That's a nice position," I said. "I quit."

I explained the promise I'd made to Judy and myself. I'm not sure he fully understood it, but we parted as friends.

I had been thinking for some time about starting my own computer services business. I had been utilizing all my talents for the benefit of CEIR, which returned the favor by demoting me. Why shouldn't I take those talents and harness them for my own benefit? I had bounced the idea off one of my best friends at CEIR, Dominic Laiti, whom I'd recruited and hired.

I liked and respected Dominic quite a bit. He was that combination of creativity and steadiness so rare in the tech sector. Every day, he left CEIR at 5 so he could have dinner with his wife and their five children. Every evening at 9, he put his kids to bed. Once that was done, he took out the work he'd brought home from the office, and he would start programming. The next morning, when he ran the programs in the office, they unfailingly worked. This was unheard of in our industry. All programs needed some degree of debugging. Not Dominic's.

Nothing riled him. His very imperturbability mystified me. I tried many times to frustrate or anger him. "Why did you do that?" I would badger. "Couldn't you have found a better way?" I was trying to ignite him, but he never once exploded. I thought, that's the guy I'd like to take with me. When I asked him to join me in launching a business, he agreed.

Control Data — one of the young industry's largest players — acquired CEIR in 1967, but I was pursuing entrepreneurship before then. And why not? I had a trusted partner. I had knowledge of the field that could match that of anybody. I had sales experience. I had a network of contacts developed through my work with ACM and AFIPS. I knew little about cash flow, business plans and revenue forecasting, but I considered myself a quick study who would pick these things up as needed.

The only important prerequisite I lacked was capital, but fortune provided me with a way to start a business without investing a penny.

9. BEWARE THE MAN WHO CRIES FROM ONE EYE

I had been an entrepreneur before.

In college, before my HoJo sojourn, I persuaded my best friends Jack Servetnick and Jerry Kramer to ante up $500 dollars apiece with me so we could rent Viola's, a hot dog stand on the boardwalk at Revere Beach, for the season. My share came from the money I was saving for the next semester. I had scouted out Viola's, and while this may not have been the most thorough due diligence, it seemed a natural to me. People loved to swim at the beach and promenade on the boardwalk. They loved hot dogs and soda pop as they promenaded. We even introduced a new product — Philly-style, thin-sliced beef sandwiches. How could we lose?

Here's how. It poured on Memorial Day and Independence Day. On two of what should have been our busiest days of the season, we sold few hot dogs, beef or anything else. I hadn't even considered what effect rain would have on Viola's sales — a major flaw in my market research. Yet the weather helped us in a completely unexpected way.

Many women who strolled along the boardwalk carried umbrellas to protect them from the rain and shield them from the hot sun. The women had to *schlep* their umbrellas to and from home, but they thought of a way to avoid that nuisance. They asked us if they could store their umbrellas at Viola's.

We may have been inexperienced kids, but we knew an opportunity when we saw one. We cleared out space in the back and introduced our new Umbrella Storage Service. We lost money on hot dogs that summer, compensated with rentals from umbrella storage and broke even on our investment, although we earned zero for our labor. If I learned nothing else from Viola's, I learned this: The marketplace will tell you what it wants, and you'd better be prepared to listen and deliver. Have options!

Viola's, though, was a youthful fling. Now, I was about to embark on an entrepreneurial journey with much more at stake. I had a family to support, and I felt responsible for Dominic and his family as well, since Dominic was abandoning a more secure job for an uncertain future with me. I had no formal business training and knew nothing of cash flow and business plans. As a result, I got kicked out of many offices trying to woo investors for our new business. Then I got an unexpected break.

Judy's brother Bob introduced me to a friend of his named Saul Feldman, who had founded and now operated a business called Heliodyne Corporation based on the West Coast. Saul had a Ph.D. in applied physics, and Heliodyne did a considerable amount of Top Secret work for the federal government on rockets — yes, it *was* rocket science — most notably for the Norton Air Force Base in San Bernardino. But Saul could see that his clients were developing greater needs for computer services; that was the added value he asked me to provide.

This was our deal. I would start and operate a Heliodyne office in Washington, DC and have an equity position in the company. What would that position be? That would be determined by how much I could grow the new office compared to the West Coast unit.

"Whatever percentage of the business you're responsible for will be yours," Saul said. "If we fall apart on the West Coast and the Washington office thrives, you'll have 100 percent of the business."

One hundred percent of the business without investing a penny? That should have been a clue that something was amiss, but I was too dazzled by my visions of golden entrepreneurship to see it at once.

*   *   *   *   *

While I was trying to build the Washington office, Saul asked me to help him with Norton Air Force Base, which wanted Heliodyne to assess the base's computer needs. As I mentioned, Saul was a physicist, and this computer work was more up my alley.

Security at the base was tight. You couldn't even land a plane there unless you were pre-registered and given prior clearance. One time, I was being flown from Van Nuys on a small, private plane which the airline forgot to register. The pilot engaged in feverish negotiations with the control tower — I was privy to it all because I was the sole passenger — when I heard the controller say: "Do not land. If you land, you land at your own risk."

Jesus Christ! We were about to be blown away by friendly fire!

Ignoring the warning, the pilot landed. As soon as we deplaned, we were surrounded by hostile MPs.

"General McCoy is waiting for me," I said.

Those were the magic words. They escorted me directly to the general. When I returned to the plane following the meeting, the MPs still were hassling the poor pilot. They were only too happy to bid us good-bye.

Brig. Gen. John L. McCoy cut an impressive figure in his uniform festooned with ribbons and brass, as befitting the head of the Titan ICBM program. (Oddly enough, he called on me later in Washington — *sans* uniform — and I didn't recognize him. He seemed a strapping six-footer in uniform, not much more than five-and-a-half feet without it.)

On one occasion when I brought him recommendations for the base's computer system, I was ushered into a conference room. McCoy sat at the head of a large table, surrounded by six or seven colonels.

I made my recommendations, one by one.

"That sounds right to me," McCoy said. "Does it sound right to you?"

"Yessir," said the first colonel.

"Yessir," said the second colonel.

"Yessir," echoed colonel No. 3.

And so on around the table. Each time I made a recommendation, the general preached, and the choir responded. I thought briefly of my notion of joining the Air Force and wondered if I'd have become the preacher or a member of the choir.

*   *   *   *   *

The contract with the Air Force was sizable, but it didn't do a thing to help grow Heliodyne's Washington office. In fact, after six months, my share of the company was worth very little because I hadn't landed a single big customer. I got plenty of calls from people wanting to join me; those were of little use until I could round up some clients.

My approach to sales generation in our high-tech business was decidedly low tech. I knocked on doors, focusing on government agencies with big budgets.

"My name is Jack Roseman, and I represent Heliodyne," I

would say as I trod the hallowed halls of federal government. "Do you need any computer programming services?"

"Another computer company?" Slam!

I reached out to contacts I'd made through the Association for Computing Machinery and was able to land some small contracts that way. It was ironic that the work I had done for ACM — which was my way of contributing to society — now was helping me keep Heliodyne afloat. It goes to show you that the good you do isn't necessarily interred with your bones.

Sheer persistence also got me a small piece of business from NASA. I knocked on the door of one contract manager repeatedly, each time to be turned away. Finally exasperated, he said:

"Roseman, I can see the only way I'm gonna get rid of you is to give you a little business. Come inside."

It was nice to be thrown a bone, but we still were struggling to get by. I didn't think we could survive without hitting at least the occasional homerun. I said as much to Dominic.

"These little contracts are getting us nowhere. So we get a $20,000 piece of business — so what? It won't sustain us, and it won't allow us to grow. Let's pursue the big fish."

"I'm with you, Jack."

"Please understand what I'm saying, Dominic. The name of this game is 'You Bet Your Company.'"

"I'm okay with that."

Shortly thereafter, we read in a government bulletin that NASA was seeking a contractor to create a centralized computer database for all the experiments sponsored by NASA facilities across the country and the world. The

Request for Proposals suggested the project would require 100 people. Given that Heliodyne's Washington office had only a handful of employees, this work seemed beyond our capabilities. So it took some *chutzpah* to submit a proposal, but submit one I did.

We didn't hear anything from NASA for a while. One day, I rolled into the office to find the entire team waiting for me. This was ominous.

"What's up, guys?"

"We don't have any inventory," Dominic said. "We don't have any work to do."

We adjourned to the conference room, wondering what we would do next and bemoaning the imminent demise of Heliodyne's Washington office. We said we would bet the company, and it looked for all the world like we'd lost our bet.

Just then, the phone rang. It was NASA inviting me to an interview the next day. As a joke to myself and the Heliodyne guys who could hear me, I played hard to get.

"Let me look at my calendar and see if I'm available. Hmmm, let me see. It looks like I *do* have a window tomorrow."

During the interview, NASA acknowledged that our proposal ranked No. 1 in technical features according to their point system. I, in turn, acknowledged that we had only five or six people.

"But you're competing against one of the largest providers in computer services," they said. I assumed this was IBM, although NASA didn't identify our chief competitor by name. "How could you ever hope to do this work with such a small staff?"

"Do you think that big company has 100 people just sitting on their hands waiting for this contract?" I countered. "They'd have to hire up. I'll get my people the same way. Moreover, whatever this contract is worth, it's a drop in the bucket to them. They have no incentive for working their asses off because they have plenty of contracts just like this one. Losing your business wouldn't hurt them. For Heliodyne, your contract would be a significant percentage of our business. You can count on us to work like crazy to deliver what you want, when you want it."

Then the *coup de grace*. I gave them my personal phone number.

"Call me at 3 AM if you need me, and I'll come. Do you think Watson would do the same?"

Thomas J. Watson, Jr., of course, was chairman and CEO of IBM and the son of IBM's founder.

Chutzpah won the day, and Heliodyne had a $4 million contract with an anchor client. Others followed. Soon, we had regular business from such important institutions as American University and the Johns Hopkins University Applied Physics Laboratory. There's a lesson in entrepreneurship here. Simply stated, it's this: If you want to be a successful entrepreneur, persevere. Be a pit bull. It's easy to give up, much harder to stay the course when you're out of clients, out of cash and out of your mind with worry. Stay the course.

Now, I was ready to build our team. With the competition among computer services providers as intense as it was, the market for programmers was fluid. We used to say that programmers could walk across the street to find a better paying job, and that was only a slight exaggeration. I formed a relationship with Halbrecht Associates (now Halbrecht

Lieberman Associates), one of the top headhunters in technology, and got plenty of sharp candidates through them and my contacts at ACM.

I'd hired people before, most notably at CEIR, but many of those employees already were in place when I got there. This was my first experience building a staff from the ground up. When I interviewed job candidates, I always thought of my mother's advice — know your customer. Their resumes usually were impeccable, their responses to standard interview questions unexceptional. So I tried to get to know them. "What is it you want from Heliodyne?" I might ask them, trying to get them to reveal something of their aspirations. I was looking for both credentials and chemistry, which always has been important to me. In fact, there have been times in my career when, if I felt employees and I didn't have the right chemistry, I offered to help them find other positions. Bad chemistry can create a miserable work environment.

When I found the right match, I offered a compensation package that was consistent with the market, but I always was amenable to a little negotiation. My rule of thumb in any negotiation is — 50 percent and then some. I'll go a little further than halfway if I can satisfy an employee. That person is more likely to work his butt off for me than one who feels he's been treated unfairly.

*   *   *   *   *

Savvy hiring was important, as was pricing our product to keep us both competitive and profitable. I developed a formula that I used to price most of our bids. I would begin with the hourly salaries of the Heliodyne people doing the work, then double that number to account for our overhead, such as fringe benefits and fixed costs. Then, I would tack on 20 percent to 30 percent — depending on the size and type of contract — for our profit. Multiply by the number of hours I thought the contract would require, and I arrived at a bid that usually kept us in the ballpark.

For smaller projects, I sometimes came up with flat fees that didn't necessarily reflect a meticulous estimation process. This got me in hot water with one of our pioneer customers.

Our contract with American University was for a project that wasn't complicated and wouldn't tie us up for long.

"How much will this cost us?" our contact at American asked.

I gave a little wave, dismissing the notion that this would be some sort of budget-buster.

"Small potatoes," I assured him.

When we finished the project, I sent him a bill for $5,000.

He showed up at my office, red faced and waving the offensive invoice.

"You told me this would be small potatoes. It's $5,000."

"In the computer business, $5,000 *is* small potatoes."

Gradually, he calmed down and was able to converse in a normal tone.

"We have another job for you, but I need to know up front what it will cost."

I took a quick look at the project outline.

"Peanuts," I said.

His face flushed even more deeply than before.

"Small potatoes. Peanuts. Stop with the food analogies and give me a firm price!"

"Five thousand," I said. "Same as before."

He cursed and protested, but he gave us the contract and paid the $5,000.

* * * * *

With my team together, I was on the prowl for business. We pursued what I thought was a good lead through Judy's cousin, a very nice guy who designed NASA's spacesuits for astronauts, a specialized trade if ever I've heard of one. The "Space Tailor," they called him. He had a friend who ran a business in Dover, Delaware. If I called on the company, he assured me, he would put in a word for me.

I made an appointment and drove from Washington, DC to Dover, maybe an hour's trip. I made my presentation to the Space Tailor's buddy and several of his associates. I could see I wasn't making an impression, so we ended it, politely but just as abruptly. Nice meeting you. We have you on file now. Dah-dee-dah. Good-bye.

It wasn't even noon yet. A typical person might have drowned his disappointment in a liquid lunch and headed home. Taking an afternoon off when there's something more to accomplish never has been my style.

I found a phone booth — yes, there were pay phones in those days — and picked up the Yellow Pages. Dover had all kinds of potential opportunities for me — a U.S. Army base, Dover Raceway. But one listing jumped out: General Foods Jell-O Division. I called Jell-O and reached the switchboard operator.

"Who's your chief financial officer?"

"That would be Mr. Williams."

"Put me through to him, please."

Mr. Williams was less than delighted to hear from me.

"Why are you bothering me with data processing? Someone who works for me is involved with that. Why don't you call him?"

So I got the name and number of the chief of computing and phoned him.

"I'm a consultant here in town — I'm not here usually," I told him. "But Mr. Williams asked me to call you to see if you need any help in computer services."

This may have been a bit of a stretch, but technically, it was true. Mr. Williams *did* ask me to call his computer guy, although it was just his way of getting rid of me. Once I invoked the name of the CFO, his subordinate couldn't hang up on me.

Turned out he did need some help, and he invited me to his office that very afternoon.

Jell-O, I discovered, was attempting to implement a new computer system for its accounting functions and having a miserable time of it. He explained the problem and objectives to me in some detail.

"Do you know anything about the Recovery Register?" he asked.

"Sure."

"Great. Do you have any questions of me?"

Did I have any questions? How could I ask questions when I knew nothing about accounting? Moreover, the language for Jell-O's new computer system was COBOL, which I had neither learned nor used. Was I facing my second major defeat of the day? I thought back to what I'd learned at Viola's. There, the market told me it wanted storage space for umbrellas rather than hot dogs. Here, the market was telling me it needed knowledge of accounting and computers.

"Send me a proposal if you're interested."

As soon as I left Jell-O, I got on the phone with Bernie Katz, Heliodyne's controller.

"Bernie," I said, "What's a Recovery Register?"

"I have no idea."

I learned later that Recovery Register had nothing to do with accounting generally but was a term specific to Jell-O that described their method of materials recovery. What I knew then and there was that I had to hire a specialist in COBOL and accounting, yet I didn't have enough knowledge of accounting to conduct useful interviews. I gave myself crash courses in accounting and COBOL and developed just enough expertise to evaluate candidates. I finally found a guy with dual expertise and experience. Ordinarily, I would not have hired him. He didn't jazz me up — no chemistry. But I needed him right away. He agreed to take the job.

"You're not an employee yet," I told him. "The way we operate, if you're here six months, you become an employee, and we'll take good care of you."

We got the Jell-O job. Six months later, my new employee-to-be buttonholed me in my office.

"I want you to know I'm quitting," he said.

"Why? We got the contract. Everything went well."

"You told me for the first six months I wouldn't be an employee. Those six months are up. If you want to hire me now, you'll have to pay me more."

"You got it," I said, seething as I said it but knowing that I needed him a little while longer.

He got his raise. A few months later, I raised him right out the door. Had his approach been a little less arrogant, I might have reacted differently, might well have gone 50 percent and then some for him. But once he tried to squeeze me, the gloves were off.

We won a renewal of the Jell-O contract without him.

* * * * *

One of the biggest priorities of the federal government during the 1960s was President Lyndon Johnson's "War on Poverty." The goals were to jump-start minority-owned businesses and create important new social service agencies for America's poor and elderly. I don't know that anyone believed we could eliminate poverty, but this vast infusion of funds could, at the very least, make a dent.

With all that cash being given away, the government wanted some sort of accountability; for that, it turned to Heliodyne. We were awarded a contract to collect and computerize follow-up reports from War on Poverty funding recipients. It was a major coup for us, but I knew it wouldn't be easy. Most follow-up reports, I suspected, would not be submitted without a little badgering. This meant I would need to spend days in the field, in some of America's toughest neighborhoods, to coax reports from reluctant organizations.

I concluded that I might need some protection in the DC area; at the recommendation of an associate, I hired a felon just released from prison for armed robbery. He put the word out that I was a good guy, merely a government contractor doing his job, and that no one should touch me. That eventually made me feel pretty confident anywhere in

Washington, but I had many other cities to visit.

In East St. Louis, I argued with a menacing-looking guy whose organization hadn't submitted its reports.

"You understand that when Washington gives you money, what they want back is a report. And we haven't gotten any reports from you."

"Fuck it, man."

"Let me tell you why you shouldn't fuck it. If you don't give reports, you won't get any more money."

"I got a 16-year-old client who's pregnant. She's supposed to be going to school. Someone's gotta take care of her. Should I do that or worry about a report for the government?"

"If you don't send the reports in, you won't help future 16-year-olds."

Sometimes that argument was persuasive, sometimes it wasn't.

In Birmingham, I stayed at the Gaston Motel, the first and only hotel or motel in the city to serve blacks and one that became part of the history of the civil rights movement. It was in Room 30 of the Gaston that Dr. Martin Luther King, Jr. and his associates formalized their plans for King to be arrested to show support for local civil rights protestors, and it was in the Gaston's courtyard that movement leaders and Alabama officials signed a peace accord. (Not everyone was happy with the compromise. On May 12, 1963, two days after the accord was signed, a pair of bombs exploded outside Room 30, damaging much of the motel's facade.) The Gaston closed down in 1986 but later was purchased by the City of Birmingham for a planned redevelopment that would commemorate the civil rights movement.

When I stayed at the Gaston, there were no sidewalks in front of the motel, so I had to slog through mud to reach the lobby. My room was illuminated by one bare light bulb that dangled from the ceiling. The only thing missing, I imagined, was a sadistic guard beating me with a rubber hose. No pictures adorned the walls, only a sign that said: "We hope you enjoyed your stay. We've spared no expense to make your stay comfortable."

At 7 PM, I walked across the street to a restaurant where, I imagined, no white man had been before. That night, at least, I was the only white diner. I began to regret not taking my street-savvy armed robber with me. Yet within 10 minutes, the patrons made me feel completely at ease. They welcomed me, joked around with me, called me "brother."

I was overwhelmed by their warmth, indeed, by the warmth of most, if not all, of the African-American communities I visited. In fact, I felt threatened only in certain Southern cities when I was traveling by car with an African-American. When we stopped for red lights, white drivers and pedestrians would shoot me looks full of daggers.

Was the War on Poverty successful? It gave birth to Medicare, Medicaid, the Job Corps, VISTA. It institutionalized food stamps, a temporary program until then. Given the slippery nature of progress in the social services area, I would call that a success. I may have been no more than a soldier in the War on Poverty, but I was pleased to do my part and learn a few things. I concluded, for example, that, though the experiences of Jews and African-Americans in the U.S. differ in many important regards, both groups have endured prejudice and poverty, which should create bonds among the victims. When African-Americans called me brother, I *felt* like their brother.

*　*　*　*　*

I was working like a demon, traveling a great deal for the War on Poverty and consequently spending very little time at our Bethesda split-level home. Once, after a particularly grueling day, I came home through the carport, which put me on the upper level. Judy was waiting for me.

"There are three people downstairs I'd like to introduce you to."

I nearly exploded.

"I just got home from work. I don't want to meet anybody. What are you doing to me?"

I walked downstairs, grumbling all the way, figuring I could say a quick hello and get the hell out of there."

"Meet Laura, Alan and Shari."

Oh boy. My wife felt the need to introduce me to our children. I was touched, embarrassed and guilty at the same time. I vowed to be a better father. Indeed, I promised Judy and the kids to spend the entire Memorial Day weekend with them.

That weekend began well enough. Judy and I got the holiday started early when we went to a movie Thursday evening. Then came the phone call. It was Bernie Katz, calling from Heliodyne's West Coast office, where he and several others were putting together a proposal.

"Jack, we really need your input for the computer end of this thing."

"I just promised my wife I would be home this weekend. I can't break that promise."

"We need you, Jack."

"Bernie. Please."

"Tell you what. Bring the family along."

I bounced it off Judy because it would be she who would be up all night washing, ironing and packing. She liked the idea — she didn't veto it, anyway — so we were on. Early Friday morning, we woke the kids and told them we all were going on a plane to California, an idea they found puzzling but exciting. We stayed at the Sportsmen's Lodge in Studio City, a lucky break for us since it was only two miles from the home of Judy's cousin, who kept all three kids one night so Judy and I could have an evening to ourselves.

It turned out to be a great weekend. We finished the proposal, and I got to spend some quality time with my family — particularly Laura. She was only 5, but when she saw the fishing pond at Sportsmen's Lodge, she wanted to catch a fish. The only marine creature I know is the wily *gefilte* fish, and there weren't any of those in the pond. Fortunately, a bystander noticed me struggling with the line and offered to assist. We spent the next few hours at it and had great fun. Our timing was terrific, too. Two years later, in 1971, fishing at the Lodge ended when an earthquake diverted the natural spring that fed the complex.

* * * * *

After a few years building Heliodyne, I was feeling pretty smug. We had won a big NASA contract, advanced the War on Poverty and solidified Jell-O, so to speak. The future looked promising. Then one day, I took a call in my office.

"I'd like to speak to Saul Feldman."

"Saul isn't here. This is Jack Roseman. Can I give him a message?"

"When you see him, just tell him that I've thought about his offer to head up Heliodyne's Washington office. I've thought about it long and hard, and I've decided not to take the job. Will you tell him that?"

I hung up the phone in a state of utter confusion. Could I believe what I'd just heard? Despite all our success, Saul had offered my job to someone else, and this guy actually told me about it, probably thinking that I knew of the offer and was preparing to take some other position within the organization. As I calmed down, I realized Saul was making his move to separate me from my equity in the company.

I stewed about it for a week or so. Saul and I were scheduled to meet. I wasted no time confronting him.

"The other day I got a phone call from a guy who said thanks but he doesn't want my job, the job you offered him."

His tears started flowing, but as I looked at Saul, I noticed something peculiar. He was crying from his right eye only. I'd never seen anything like it, and the sight of it made me even more furious.

"Let me tell you what I want from you. I need an agreement from you, in writing, stipulating that if I leave this position, Heliodyne must close its Washington office and not open another one without my permission. That goes whether I resign or you kick me out. No DC office without my authorization."

I still was so shaken that I called Bernie Katz, the man who knew Saul best. I began to recount our conversation when he interrupted me.

"Let me guess," Bernie said. "He cried from one eye."

Saul gave me the written agreement I asked for. I really wanted to stay with Heliodyne — I'd built it from scratch, and I'd invested a lot of myself in its growth. But the atmosphere was toxic now. It was time to move on. I shared the whole sorry story with Dominic; we began to make plans to launch another company.

Shortly thereafter, Saul sold Heliodyne to KMS Industries, named for its founder and CEO, Keeve Milton "Kip" Siegel. Since I'd managed to retain my equity, I realized some cash from the sale, but it wasn't a big payday. Over time, KMS focused its energy on the generation of power from laser fusion, a process it demonstrated successfully in the lab but one that never proved replicable or scalable. Although KMS won several government contracts, it found itself limping along on the proceeds from a life insurance policy purchased by Siegel, who died young but had the foresight to name KMS his beneficiary. It wasn't enough, and the company failed in 1993.

Saul Feldman went to work for KMS but had to extricate himself from several lawsuits filed by Bernie Katz, who alleged that Saul had promised that Bernie would operate the new entity created by the KMS purchase of Heliodyne. The suits ping-ponged their way through the California court system, where verdicts were overturned and cases remanded. It was enough to make a grown man cry.

From one eye.

Lena, Hy and Jack's mother,
Bessie Roseman, in Ukraine.

Jack's father, Abraham
Roseman, in Ukraine.

Bessie Roseman (center back) and Hy (center front) arriving
at Ellis Island.

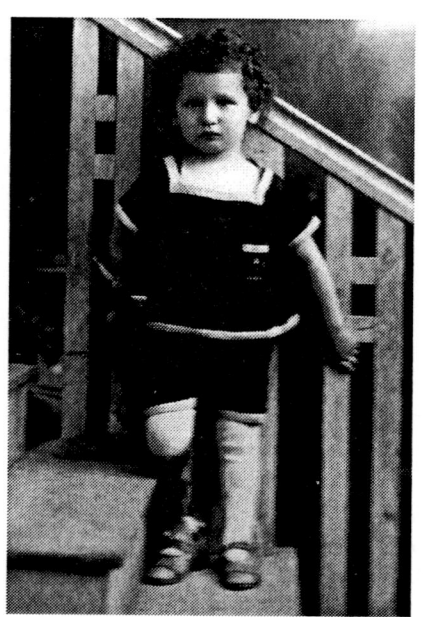

Hy Roseman.

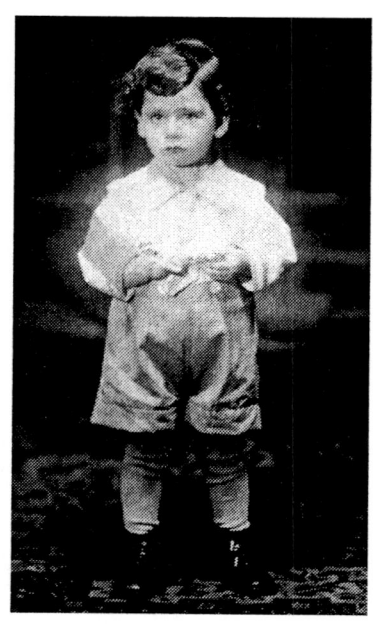

Jack Roseman.

*Children of Jack's brother
Leibel in Ukraine.*

*Jack's Uncle Morris Roseman
a.k.a. Juste Maurice.*

Jack with his parents (left to right) Bessie, Jack and Abraham Master's Degree, 1955.

Judy Rosenthal.

Jack and Judy Roseman on their wedding day.

Jack and the IBM 650 at General Electric- Schenectady, NY.

The Roseman family- (left to right) Alan, Judy, Jack, Laura and Shari.

Happy Evelyn and her foal, Actron.

John Godfrey and Jack (On-Line Systems-Pittsburgh, PA).

Laura, Alan and Shari (2002).

*Jack and Judy with their grandchildren (left to right) Brooke,
Paige, Judy, Jack, Kyle, Sheena and Faylyn (2013).*

Jack, in his study, with a vacuum tube from the original Whirlwind II.

Jack and Judy Roseman (2017).

Bronze sculpture by Michael Kraus commissioned by Jack Roseman in 1988 for Temple Ohav Shalom Holocaust Memorial Garden in remembrance of the brother he never met. Leibel (whose name is rendered in the sculpture with an alternate spelling) and his family were among the 6 million Jews who perished in the Holocaust. (Photos courtesy of Ira Russo).

10. IN WHICH I BECOME PRESIDENT OF GENERAL MOTORS (NOT QUITE, BUT ON-LINE SYSTEMS WILL HAVE TO BE CLOSE ENOUGH)

Xonics.

That was the name of the new company Dominic and I, as well as some of our Heliodyne colleagues, wanted to start. As we envisioned it, Xonics would be like Heliodyne, but it would take computer data processing to a much higher level where we could target such customers as the Department of Defense and face little competition. We imagined that the contracts we'd be pursuing would be lucrative. A number of people from Heliodyne's West Coast office, including Bernie Katz, the controller who ended up suing Saul Feldman, indicated they would be part of the Xonics team, giving us a nucleus of senior executives in technology and business.

Xonics did indeed launch, but it did so without me. While we were planning the launch, I got a call from John Godfrey, my old friend from GE. I really liked and respected John. We got along so well that Judy and I once vacationed with John and his family at Lake George in New York's Adirondack Mountains. We spent a week in a cabin shortly after Judy and I were married — and Judy was pregnant with Laura.

John was from Michigan and earned his undergraduate and graduate degrees from Michigan State University, but you would have mistaken him for an Englishman: analytical, laconic, seemingly imperturbable, although I later learned that the demands of operating a business could tie him up in knots. If you gave him a paper clip and asked him what it was, he would hold it this way and peer at it, hold it that way and peer some more. Finally, after perhaps several minutes, he would pronounce, "I believe this is a paper clip." He was that thorough, that reluctant to jump to conclusions. He and I were polar opposites in that regard, so I knew if we worked together, he would brake my impulsiveness while I could prompt him to faster decisions.

He also was, shall we say, thrifty. When he was on the road and needed gas, he never would buy it on a turnpike or other major highway. He'd exit the turnpike and look for some small-town pump, figuring he'd save a few pennies per gallon. When we vacationed with the Godfreys, we did not eat one meal out because John wouldn't tolerate the expense. Instead, we brought in provisions and ate in the cabin. Judy and John's wife, Velda, whipped up a huge vat of potato salad that we ate with every meal. Judy got so sick of potato salad that, for some months thereafter, she couldn't bear to even walk by the deli counter at the supermarket. (John didn't seem to mind, however, when I purchased a bottle of Drambuie, which we found a whole lot more satisfying than the potato salad. "Very expensive mouthwash," he called it.)

John had made his bones, on Wall Street and in the tech sector, with an early computer game he designed called Dr. Nim, a variation on the ancient Asian game of nim. The plastic Dr. Nim unit held a tube of 15 marbles. If you were challenging Dr. Nim, you picked anywhere from one to three marbles; Dr. Nim then would do the same. If there was only one marble left when it was your turn to choose, you lost. The rolling of the marbles activated the "computer" and guided Dr. Nim's selections. The set also included an instructional manual outlining successful strategies for beating Dr. Nim as well as a tutorial on computers. A company called E.S.R., Inc. marketed Dr. Nim as an educational toy, selling for about $3.50 per unit. If you troll on-line exchange sites today, you'll find Dr. Nim units in good condition selling for about $45.

Dr. Nim was a smash throughout the late '60s, handsomely rewarding John and his backers, which included Ladenburg Thalmann, a prestigious old Wall Street brokerage and investment bank that has been a New York Stock Exchange member since 1879. At a meeting where John was briefing Ladenburg Thalmann on the success of Dr. Nim, they asked him to crystal ball the future and reveal the next big thing. John was only too happy to oblige.

"Let me tell you what I think is coming down," he said. "It's called computer time-sharing."

John went on to explain that, as he saw the immediate future, computing in the business arena was about to enter a new phase. Companies no longer needed to spend zillions to purchase and program their own computers. Instead, they could buy just as much computer time as they needed from vendors who would shoulder the burden of operating and maintaining the computers. Time-sharing, he told them, would be the state of the art.

How much would he need to start a time-sharing company? About $300,000, John said, expecting to be hooted from the room. But there was no sticker shock here. The investors had done well with John and Dr. Nim, and $300,000 was trivial for these heavy hitters. One of the Ladenburg Thalmann group suggested that he had solid corporate connections in Pittsburgh; if John based his start-up there, those connections would give the company a leg up. That's how On-Line Systems, Inc. was born, and that's how Pittsburgh became its headquarters.

John had his vision. He had his concept. He had his investors. What he didn't have was the inclination to build a business from the ground up. For that, he brought in a former colleague of his at GE and named him On-Line's president. As it turned out, John and his old colleague were like oil and water, and On-Line soon was without a president once more. John needed someone who knew computers, someone who shared John's enthusiasm for this new phase of computer development, and, most of all, someone he could trust.

He called me.

"Jack," he said, "I need you."

Those are the magic words to me. Promise me fame and fortune and I'm cynical and a tough sell. But when a friend says he needs me, I'm a pushover. As John laid out his plan, I found myself agreeing with nearly every point. The technology John envisioned greatly interested me because I could see it was the wave of the future. A company didn't need to spend $1 million for its own computer and peripherals. How much time on the mainframe do you need? Ten minutes? Half hour? That's what you'll be charged for. Computer time could be sold like electricity. You don't own a generator to provide your electricity, right? You flip a switch, the utility sends electricity to you and you're charged only for the amount of power you use. Soon, companies would purchase computer time just as they did commodities.

The peripherals were cheap — a phone and a modem to connect you to the computers, a Flexowriter in your office to print the output. And if the Flexowriter wasn't fast enough for you, just add your own printer to the mix.

John was pioneering the model that would dominate business computing for the next decade or so until some sonofagun named Steve Jobs introduced the notion that you could package all the computer power you needed in a small machine that sat on your desktop.

On-Line Systems was where I wanted to be. I left Xonics before it launched and made plans to join Godfrey at On-Line's Pittsburgh headquarters. Leaving Dominic wasn't easy. We had been together through CEIR and Heliodyne; I had come to count on his friendship and steadiness, and I believe those feelings were mutual. I know he would have been an asset in helping me build On-Line, and I know he would have accepted a position if I'd offered one. But I also knew that if he kept following me, like an assistant coach tagging along with his manager, he would forever have been in my shadow, and he was too talented an executive, too fine a person to remain in the background his entire career. He might not have appreciated my decision, he might not appreciate it to this day, but Dominic had earned his wings.

And soar he did. He left Xonics after a time and, with a group of investors, purchased Hadron, Inc., a government systems consulting company, and did well enough to build his family a splendid estate in Virginia. He became the Dominic Laiti I knew he could be. We've stayed in touch over the years, which I hope is an indication that he understands why I didn't offer him a position at On-Line.

* * * * *

As On-Line's new president, I was hip deep in the company from Day 1, working 18-hour days, seven-day weeks. Yet there was one little personal matter that required attention: we had to move from Bethesda to Pittsburgh . . . and quickly. The burden of the move fell to Judy, and what a nightmare it became.

We knew we needed to live in Pittsburgh's northern suburbs, since that's where On-Line was headquartered, and we knew we needed a first-rate special education program so that Alan could continue his speech therapy. In Maryland, Montgomery County had a program that was ideal for Alan, but what would be available in Pittsburgh? Judy made three trips to Pittsburgh to research special education in Allegheny County as well as available homes in the North Hills. She determined that only the North Hills School District offered an appropriate special education program. So the general locale was settled, but was there a suitable home for us in the school district?

On her third trip, Judy met with a realtor and gave him our specifications: four bedrooms, an office, North Hills School District. Was anything like that available? The realtor flipped through his index cards and found precisely one such house on the market.

"I'd like to go see it," Judy said.

"When you're husband's in town, give me a call."

Was that ever the wrong response. He got an earful and realized his blunder. He took Judy to the home in Ross Township. It met our needs, although it lacked central air conditioning and any sort of organized landscaping. Judy and I discussed the house and figured we probably couldn't do better, given our requirements and time constraints. We put in a bid and got the house. We were all set to move into a home I'd never seen. This may seem like a case of misplaced priorities — who moves into a house he's never seen? But it had a certain logic to it. I was seldom home; Judy was there all the time. So if the house suited her, it suited me.

 The odyssey for Judy and the kids wasn't over. On the day our relocation was scheduled, movers in Allegheny County were on strike. They wouldn't move anything across the county line. So we had to ship the bulk of our furniture to a Pittsburgh warehouse, where it would remain for three weeks. Judy packed everything else — Laura, Alan, Shari, the bird, our clothes, our houseplants, air mattresses (our beds were in the warehouse) and a six-foot folding table that she could use as a platform for wallpapering — into our station wagon. Once she got everyone safely into the home, she bought a refrigerator — we didn't know how long the strike would last, and we needed something for food storage until then — and began wallpapering like crazy.

*   *   *   *   *

When I took over as president, On-Line's computer center was tiny, occupying a small, nondescript building off McKnight Road, one of the major arteries in the North Hills. The center housed one or two computers, which may not seem like much, but these were million-dollar units that together could service from 25 to 50 clients, depending on how much mainframe time those clients needed. But we wouldn't have much capacity for growth without additional computers.

John set out to address that, although it took a few years. We purchased land on Evergreen Drive — probably a mile from our existing computer center — and constructed two buildings to serve as our new computer center and corporate headquarters. John masterminded the project, and he did a magnificent job creating state-of-the-art facilities for us. Next, John prepped our computer vendor, Digital Equipment Corporation, so that they would be poised to provide any new units we needed — including PDP-10s, which were the workhorses, and PDP-11s, smaller units that managed traffic. John and I worked with our technical and sales people to estimate what our needs would be. This was a critical step because the lead-time for a new PDP-10 was anywhere from six months to a year, including the time we needed to de-bug it.

John never hesitated to order a new computer if he thought there was the slightest chance we might need it. Extra capacity was preferable to no flexibility for growth or customers angry about lengthy response times.

*　*　*　*　*

The Rosemans had their home, and On-Line Systems had its infrastructure. We were ready for big things. But there still were tricky waters to navigate. One was the relationship between current employees and their new president. On-Line at this point had about a dozen employees who'd been with the start-up a little more than a year; they'd all been reporting directly to John, the chairman. Now, their access to John was more limited, as they had to run everything through me. This did not go down well. On more than one occasion, I found employees doing exactly the opposite of what I'd directed. John, they told me, had authorized it.

This rankled me, but more important than that, it was inimical to the success of the company. My employees were smart, technically savvy people, the kind of people who can be tough to manage. Once engineers develop a new mousetrap, they're keen to work on it the rest of their lives because they always can think of slight improvements. Let's add code here. Change the cheese from Swiss to cheddar. My attitude was, unless I can charge the customer more for your tweaks, it's a waste of time that won't help us.

Yet John was undermining my authority and indulging their vanity. I marched into his office to confront him.

"Do you want me to quit? Because if you keep overruling my decisions, that's what I'll have to do."

"I won't do it again."

"That's the third time you've told me that."

John seldom revealed his feelings, but this time, his voice filled with emotion.

"I never told you this, Jack, but before you came, I used to go home for lunch every day and vomit. That's how much I hate managing. Since you came here, I haven't vomited once. If you leave, I'm right behind you."

So much for the John Godfrey stiff upper lip.

"Then here's the way it has to be. When they bring something to you, you say, 'You'll have to ask Jack.'"

I knew this was only the first step in legitimizing my authority. You can order employees to obey the company president, but that doesn't mean they buy in. To achieve that, I modified and expanded the techniques I'd used at CEIR and Heliodyne to solicit employee input.

I made it a habit to walk around the office at least once a week and talk to employees. I would ask: "If you were president of this company, what would you do? What policy or practice would you implement? Give me one suggestion, and I'll tell you whether I'll do it or not. If I won't do it, I'll tell you why. And if I have to think about it, I'll get back to you." My primary purpose was to get some great ideas from employees who were hands on with our computers and our customers. But this technique also was a morale booster — here was the president of the company wanting *my* advice. The key to the success of the "walk around" is follow up. If you solicit recommendations and don't follow up, the whole exercise is for nil. Your employees will see through you.

I remember flat-out rejecting only one employee suggestion — that On-Line give some of our people multiyear contracts. My strong sense was that committing all that money up front would have been highly dangerous for a young company.

"Let me get this straight," I responded. "You're asking me for something I don't even give my wife. All she knows is, we're married today. She doesn't know if I'll file for divorce tomorrow."

Of course, it was much more likely that Judy would divorce her workaholic husband, but they didn't need to know that.

I was a hands-on president in several other ways. The computers operated 24 hours a day, so we had people working 24 hours a day. I wanted all the shifts to know me. How could I do that with the midnight shift? Be there. I often used my late-night time with them to stress our emphasis on good customer service. My rule was: Our phones must be answered by the second ring. At times, when I woke up in the middle of the night, I used my disrupted sleep as an opportunity to phone the computer center. If there was no answer after two rings, I slammed my phone down, got dressed and went to work.

"Where's the fire," I would ask. "I know there must be a fire here or you would have answered the phone before the third ring."

It didn't take long for them to get to know me — and how serious I was about customer service. So when I said these things, they knew I would check.

I was particularly tough on our sales reps — we had them in every major city. I didn't want our sales people in the office from 9 to 5. They needed to be knocking on doors, wooing prospects, making follow-up calls. I was a stickler on this. I would call our sales offices during the day and ask for the sales rep. God pity him if he answered the phone. For all that, I did a bum job generally in recruiting sales people. My batting average was about .500. If I wanted three sales people, I needed to look for six.

The first sales rep that John hired, before I arrived on the scene, was Dave Groutt. Dave was a good guy — we became friends eventually — but he hated making cold calls. To reach my office, I had to pass his desk. Each time I saw him sitting there, my blood boiled. Finally, I took to leaving a dollar bill on his desk whenever I found him sitting there.

"What's this all about?" he asked.

"Do me a favor," I said. "Take the dollar and go to the movies. That way, I can tell myself you're out making sales calls. But if I see you here, I know you're not making calls, and it's pissing me off."

My ploy didn't really inspire him to change his approach, so we agreed to disagree. Dave stayed at On-Line until its sale, then came with me when I operated Actronics.

*   *   *   *   *

Yet another potential land mine was On-Line's board of directors. I'd never really had to deal with a board or outside investors before since CEIR and Heliodyne were closely held and, of course, I was one of Heliodyne's owners. This was a new situation for me. On-Line's board and investors were Wall Street veterans. In these matters, I was a rookie, and I needed to get up to speed fast.

Soon after I signed on, a man named Buddy Erpf invited John and me to a session in New York, sort of a meet-and-greet for the new guy. Although Buddy was not formally on our board, he was the president of Ladenburg Thalmann and ably represented on our board by a number of Ladenburg Thalmann people. Plus, he was an On-Line investor holding a significant number of our shares.

By way of introduction, Buddy told me: "I don't trust anyone unless he first proves to me I can." Was this a warning to me to toe his line? Things got stranger still when, while the three of us were dining at an elegant New York restaurant, Buddy offered me a percentage of the company. He knew I already had equity — that was a condition of my employment — but this would be an additional piece taken from his holdings.

The warning bells sounded in my head. What was Erpf's game, offering me equity when he knew I already had it? Was he trying to buy my loyalty to him personally? Hedging his bet on John by establishing a direct pipeline to me? Neither of those possibilities appealed to me.

"Why would you do that?" I asked.

"Because I want you under my thumb," he said, grinding his thumb into the top of the table to make sure I got the point. I did.

"As far as I'm concerned, lunch is done. There's not enough tea in China to buy me."

I walked out. A couple minutes later, John caught up with me.

"You know, Jack, for two cents I'd have said the same thing."

"You should have told me; I'd have given you two cents."

As meet-and-greets go, this one was pretty revealing. I learned about Buddy's need for control; he saw a little of the Roseman defiance. We didn't speak for months after that incident, but I knew I had made an important enemy.

There was more to come. A few years later, after On-Line had enjoyed some success and was growing apace, Mark

Finkel, whose father was a retired investment banker who sat on our board, invited Judy and me to New York to enjoy a night of theater with him and his wife. After we'd dined at a fine restaurant, he said:

"Why don't you and I go back to my apartment and let the girls go to the theater?"

I didn't like the sound of this at all, and seeing his set-up nearly unnerved me. We rode an elevator that opened smack dab in the middle of his apartment. Been to a lot of fancy places, but that's the only time I've seen that. Young Finkel quickly got down to business.

"We think Godfrey is holding you back," he said. "We think On-Line Systems would go further without him. We'll take care of John very well financially, but we want you to take over as chairman."

I may have been stunned by the grandeur of his apartment, but I wasn't so awed that I didn't see his offer for what it was: appalling.

"You should know this," I said. "The last day of John Godfrey at On-Line Systems is my last day. I wouldn't be at On-Line but for John. Don't touch him. He started this company, and forcing him out would hurt him personally. I can't do that."

The ironic thing was, his assessment of John may have been spot on. John was a visionary, an entrepreneur if you will, but once a company reached operating mode, John may have been miscast as an administrator. But I hated the approach, the intrigue and the treachery of it. I hated that the move had come from Mark Finkel, whose father had become such a close friend of mine that he stayed with Judy and me whenever he was in Pittsburgh for board meetings.

Some years later, I had the opportunity to serve on the boards of a number of tech start-ups. Wiser from my experiences with On-Line's board, I tried to be open and helpful rather than cook up back-room deals disguised as theater parties. That is so not me.

*   *   *   *   *

Computer time-sharing became a hot space. I don't know that anyone ever counted all the players — I could name the major ones — but I read recently that more than 100 companies offered computer time-sharing. With that kind of congestion, we needed big, multiyear contracts if we were to grow and succeed, and we got more than our share of them. One was with the United States Senate. Most mail sent out by senators — and you know what kind of volume that represents — was generated at our computer center in Pittsburgh before being printed for mailing in Washington. Even when you won business like that, you couldn't rest. You snare a $1 million contract, great! But if it goes away, you need another $1 million contract just to replace it. We were always in sales mode, and the pressure was intense.

It occurred to me that if the domestic market was so competitive, perhaps we should explore the international arena. We got our opportunity when we bid for a company called Dynabank that produced software for banks that weren't big enough to create their own. Mellon Bank, Continental Illinois National Bank and First National Bank of Atlanta —the owners of Dynabank — said they would entertain our offer only if we established a London office, since many of the company's clients were in the UK and elsewhere in Europe. We could have launched a company or division in the UK, but my analysis told me it would be cheaper and quicker to buy a small company. After a rather hurried search, I found one: a small Reliance Insurance

Company unit that worked in the data processing space. Reliance wanted to divest the unit in the wake of the company's takeover by Saul Steinberg, the financier and corporate raider who became infamous for his "greenmail" technique. Data processing wasn't exactly our sweet spot, but the Reliance company would give us our British beachhead and, at $300,000, the purchase price was right.

I was still on the prowl for a significant UK acquisition. The head of our UK unit suggested a possible target for us. It was called Atkins Group, which was started and owned by Sir William Atkins and had grown to become the largest engineering consulting company in the UK. It was headquartered south of London in Epsom, home of Epsom salts and the Epsom Derby. Atkins had launched a consulting subsidiary called Atkins Computing and was looking to sell it to raise cash for the parent company. It was a great fit for On-Line, but we were late to the party. One of our chief rivals, Tymshare, Inc., already had made an offer that Atkins liked in principle. All that remained was for paperwork to be reviewed and signed.

Even at that late date, they agreed to see me. I made the trip to Epsom to meet with Phillip Worthington, who was Sir William's son-in-law, and "the troika," the three guys who ran Atkins Computing. Phillip asked if I wanted to see their P&L and other financial pro forma.

"Here's what I need," I said. I pointed to the troika. "Let me spend an hour or two with them. My relationship with them is the most important part of this deal. If they don't like me, I don't want the company no matter what the books say. If they like me and if I like them, I really would like to see the books."

This was not some clever sales pitch. To me, all businesses

are, at heart, people businesses. In this transaction in particular, the interpersonal chemistry was more important than the numbers. Indeed, after we spent some time together, it looked like the chemistry was there. I wanted to make them an offer then and there before they signed off with Tymshare. But I had one more obstacle to overcome: my board.

When I proposed the purchase to my board, I was expecting a rubber-stamp approval. They had other ideas. That little Reliance unit we'd purchased for $300,000 was losing money, and the board was afraid we were throwing good money after bad. They voted. I lost.

This was an unacceptable outcome. Buddy Erpf had his taste of the Roseman defiance. Now it was the board's turn.

"This is a good deal, and I've put a lot of myself into it," I said. "Either we buy Atkins Computing or you're telling me, Jack, why don't you go. And I'll go, no problem. You might want to take another vote."

Even as I said it, I realized I had transformed this business matter into a vote of confidence on Roseman's leadership. I also knew that I had ventured into the board's den several times already and been lucky to come away with my body parts intact. Still, I felt that strongly about the Atkins deal and was ready to walk away if they disagreed.

They voted again, this time approving the purchase. After the meeting, one of the board members, a man named John Heimerdinger who was part of the Ladenburg Thalmann faction, found me in my office. John and I ultimately became great friends . . . but not that day.

"If you ever do that again," he said, "I *will* vote against you."

Even with the board's approval to pursue the deal, it proved stubbornly difficult to close. I tried to pressure Dennis Chandler, president of Atkins Computing (and one of the troika), to accelerate matters, but I was getting nowhere, it seemed. We were probably several months into the process when Chandler called me.

"Sir William has no plans for tomorrow afternoon," he said. "Why don't you have a spot of tea with him?"

That's exactly the way he said it, a spot of tea.

"Can you assure me that he'll see me tomorrow afternoon?"

"I'll make sure he's available."

I flew to England that night and met the following afternoon with Sir William. I didn't know how much time I had with him, so I cut to the chase.

"Sir William, the chief benefit of this sale to us is your people. If you don't make up your mind to sell this company, they'll leave and you'll have nothing to sell."

"How do I know you'll take good care of them?"

"I know we'll work well together. I'm not concerned."

"We'll make the deal."

And that was it. I don't think the meeting lasted more than 30 minutes. I did spend more time with Sir William after the deal closed and he invited Judy and me to his estate — an endless expanse of grass, beautiful horses grazing, someone shouting for "Billy." It was his wife, of course. I suppose I shouldn't have expected her to call him Sir William, but "Billy" was a little jarring.

There still were plenty of open issues; Sir William designated Phillip Worthington to work those out with me. Phillip taught me a lesson in negotiations that I'll never forget. Here was his game: We'd review all the open issues and check off those that weren't settled. Then we would try to resolve the unresolvables. When we came to a difference of opinion, I would say, "Okay, on this one, I give in." I might do the same for the next one, thinking that Phillip would yield on the next item or two. But he didn't.

"Why don't we put this one in the basket?" he said. "We'll look at the basket when we're all done."

By the time we got to the basket, I had done all the compromising. When we emptied the issues in the basket, Phillip expected me to compromise on half of them, too. The bottom line: I yielded on probably 75 percent of the open issues thanks to Phillip and his basket. I give Phillip all the credit in the world for his cleverness, but I also fault myself for being naïve and too eager to close the deal.

All that remained was to button down the details with the two sets of lawyers — Atkins' lawyers and On-Line's counterparts. When we sat down to do that, our progress was frustratingly slow, so slow that it looked as though it might take us all night.

"I have an early-morning flight," I announced. "If we're not done by then, I'm going home and the deal is off."

Things were getting tense. Then I remembered the beer. When she traveled abroad with me, Judy always searched for exotic beer cans that I could add to my collection; on this trip, she found three or four six packs that I happened to have with me. At some point, I would need to empty the contents — from the bottom, to preserve the attractiveness and value of the cans. Why not do it now and achieve two objectives — empty the contents and relieve some of the tension in the room?

"Anybody want a beer?"

The lawyers accepted my offer and watched in amazement while I opened the cans from the bottom, poured the beer into glasses and passed the glasses around. When I offered a second round, though, they demurred, accusing me of trying to get them drunk. I have to admit that had our positions been reversed — some crazy Brit trying to buy my company while emptying beer cans from the bottom — I would have been just as suspicious.

We got the deal done, and I made my flight. We ended up paying a combination of cash and On-Line stock for Atkins Computing; our new division was so successful for us it paid for itself within 18 months. And of course, we were able to complete the acquisition of Dynabank, the deal that had triggered all the *mischegas*.

I was true to my word to Sir William. We made sure his people were comfortable with their new employer. I became especially close with Dennis Chandler. On one of my trips to England, the troika took me to a pub — first time I'd experienced that. The pint and kidney pie were okay, but I really enjoyed the camaraderie.

Some time after the deal closed, the troika were in Pittsburgh for an On-Line staff meeting and had some time to kill on a Sunday. They decided to experience something totally American — a flea market. Imagine their surprise when they ambled through the Wildwood Flea Market and spied their boss, Jack Roseman, esteemed President of On-Line Systems, Inc., hawking 50-cent beer can collectibles from a folding table. We all laughed about it and became even closer, although I don't remember their buying any beer cans.

*   *   *   *   *

When I became its president, On-Line Systems already was

traded on the NASDAQ. But Ladenburg Thalmann used its clout to get the company listed on the American Stock Exchange. Being on the AMEX was a big boost, giving us a higher profile and potentially more investors. It also brought me closer to my childhood goal of running a company, preferably General Motors, that traded on the New York Stock Exchange. That goal seemed more achievable than ever.

Through Ladenburg Thalmann's good offices, I became the first person to buy On-Line shares on the AMEX. On Nov. 24, 1970, I purchased 100 shares at 8-1/2. It was a moment of great pride for me — I framed the purchase ticket and have it still.

Yet along with that pride came an even greater sense of responsibility. I worked virtually round the clock. I fretted the stock price, worrying about even the slightest drop. But my biggest fear was that we would lose a customer and not be able to continue our growth curve, which, of course, would drive down our share price. All this was taking a toll on me. I passed the point of rationality, although I certainly couldn't have said that at the time. Here's the sequence that brought things to a head.

We had a seven-figure contract with the University of Pittsburgh to provide computer services for their cancer research. Things went well, and we got a Request for Proposals from the National Institutes of Health, which was funding the research, for the next phase. As we were preparing our proposal, something strange happened. A number of our computer operators reported to me that they had received feelers from Pitt to work on the very project for which On-Line was bidding. It was pretty clear that Pitt made its own pitch to NIH and cut On-Line out of the equation, and just as clear that Pitt had received very encouraging signals from NIH. As if that weren't enough, the Pitt executive trying to steal our employees was the very same man I succeeded as On-Line's president.

I was incensed. I went to Pitt and met with the vice chancellor in charge of Pitt's end of the project.

"Let me tell you something," I said. "The University of Pittsburgh exists only because corporations like On-Line Systems pay taxes that support you. Now I find you're competing with us? If I have to, I'll give speeches and hold press conferences to let the public know what you're doing."

"This is private research, Jack."

"Bullshit. It's like being in the business of making prophylactics and calling it research on birth control. So don't tell me this. But I will make you a promise. I intend to handcuff you to my wrist. If I fall off the cliff, you'll fall, too."

Outrageous, irrational, over the top . . . but I wasn't done. I spent the next few days on the phone, bitching to legislators — state and federal — about Pitt's betrayal. I stayed up all night writing follow-up letters to those lawmakers. Finally, I flew to Washington to meet with, among other people, the NIH contract administrator. I ranted and raved, called him anti-business and a few other choice terms. He looked at me coldly.

"If the University of Pittsburgh doesn't get this contract," he said, " I guarantee you won't." (He was a man of his word. We learned several weeks later that another bidder won the contract. Pitt and On-Line *did* fall off the cliff together.)

Exhausted from several days without sleep, finally spent of my righteous indignation, I flew back to Pittsburgh. I made it to the terminal and felt a demon I thought I had exorcised years ago. I phoned Judy.

"Get a cab and meet me in front of the airport. I don't think I can drive."

But I already had driven myself—to another bleeding ulcer, with even bumpier highway ahead.

11. HALF A HEART ONWARD

The bleeding ulcer turned out to be a minor setback. I took maybe a week off work and felt fine again. The next sequence of medical misadventures was anything but minor. It took a decade to play out, changed me physically forever and forced me to take a look at my life — indeed life, in general — through new lenses. I like to think of this period as a drama, a near-tragedy in three acts.

Act 1 — Heart Attack

My normal weight was in the 170-pound range, but over the course of several years, I had ballooned up over 200 pounds. Bob Donovan, my primary care physician and good friend, ordered me to lose weight or risk a heart attack. I went on a serious diet, and Judy did everything she could to help me. We took a vacation in Florida and ate red snapper every night — no red meat. Once home, we continued to live almost exclusively on fish. I lost 20 pounds, but in 1973, at the age of 42, I had a heart attack anyway. (For years, I teased Donovan about how lousy his advice was. His response was always the same: if I hadn't lost that weight, the heart attack might well have been fatal.)

I was in bed on a Sunday morning in March — just another workday for me — but when I awoke, things didn't feel quite right. There was no pain, but I was tired. Judy was preparing to leave the house for a temple meeting and was amazed to find me still in bed.

"Aren't you going to work?"

"I'm a little tired today. I think I'll nap for a while, then go to the office a little later."

By mid-morning, I wasn't feeling any better, and my

breathing was labored. I was alone in the house.

I found Alan outside playing baseball on the street.

"Where's Laura?"

"Next door."

"Tell her to come over right away."

When she arrived, I explained the situation to her. She may have been only 11, but she was level headed and responded like a champ. She phoned Donovan, who advised her to call the police to get me to the hospital, where he would meet us. Laura and our neighbor, Bill Kiser, contrived to get the police there. There were no ambulances in Ross Township then, so the police rushed me to North Hills Passavant Hospital in the back of a station wagon.

Donovan was there when I arrived, and Judy, plucked from her meeting by Kiser, got there a few minutes later. Once the doctors determined I'd had a heart attack, they put me upstairs in the intensive care unit. What was amazing to me was that I remained alert and pain free. But I could tell from the looks on the faces of my wife and my doctor that this was serious. When Donovan left the room briefly, I whispered to Judy:

"As soon as possible, when you get a chance, buy Bob a nice briefcase. He's been great."

It was as if by focusing on a professional courtesy, I could shove this rude intrusion out of my life. It didn't work, and I finally passed out.

I learned later that my condition was much more critical than I supposed. We never did figure out whether the chief culprit in my heart attack was arterial blockages or a spasm. Since I was essentially asymptomatic, a spasm might be the more likely explanation. Wouldn't I have experienced some symptoms if the blood flow to my heart had been diminishing steadily?

In any case, the facts were stark. The right rear segment of my heart no longer functioned; it was dead. Donovan broke the news to Judy: I might not survive the night.

But I did — and I kept on surviving, thanks in no small part to Judy's dedication and companionship. She was with me in intensive care — for as long as she was permitted to stay — and throughout the duration of my hospitalization, which stretched to about three weeks. Judy's mother came to stay with the kids. Judy brought them to the hospital several times to see me. I still have a photograph — one I cherish — of Alan, who was 8 at the time, lying in my hospital bed with me.

Both Lena and Hy visited me. While he was there, Hy leaned over my bed and whispered: "You don't have to worry about making a name for us. It's okay if the name Roseman doesn't mean anything to the world." O Hy, my brother, my friend, my role model. You already let that genie out of the bottle. Too late to stuff him back in.

Indeed, I was still in intensive care when I began to fret about work. I asked Judy to get me a tape recorder so I could dictate some memos to the staff. When she discussed it with Donovan, he decided it would be better to allow me to do it than to deny me the opportunity and perhaps raise my stress level.

So I recorded memos, which Judy dutifully took to my secretary. Then she would meet with John Godfrey, who would use another tape recorder to provide me with briefings that I devoured as soon as Judy returned to the hospital. John's reports were thorough and meticulous —

often 30 minutes long — just as you would expect from John, and I very much appreciated them. They made me feel I was still in the loop.

My health problems were quite an ordeal for Judy. She was always on the go, shunting between the hospital and On-Line, trying to catch up with her mother and the kids when she could. (These days, whenever I'm in the hospital, Judy tells the staff that she'll be staying overnight with me. She insists on doing this because she says I'm too polite and proud to ring for the nurses when I need them. That reduces the wear and tear on her, but back then, the hospital wouldn't allow family to stay overnight.) When I got back on my feet, I asked her what the toughest part was for her. Her answer surprised me.

"I never knew what to say when you asked me how On-Line was doing," she said. "If I told you the stock was down, you'd have been worried and depressed. If I told you it was up, it would have appeared that the business was getting along fine without you, and you'd have been worried and depressed."

My secretary printed all the memos I dictated and saved them. Years later, I found the pile and reread the memos. They were as trivial as could be. Here were things I was sure needed my attention — even while I was playing hide and seek with Death — and not one of them meant a thing. This gives you some sense of how my perspective would change.

*   *   *   *   *

After leaving the hospital, I recuperated at home for several weeks. Without work to occupy me, I had no idea what to do with myself. I'd always wondered how I would look with a beard. This was the perfect time to try it because if the experiment failed, few people would see the disastrous results. Sure enough, even though my hair was still brown, my beard came in a salt-and-pepper color that, I was advised by certain parties close to me, made me look older. So I kept the mustache, shaved the beard.

We had a beautiful spring that year, and I noticed that our backyard, which we'd landscaped, was infested with moles. A slew of them. I asked Judy to get me a BB gun so I could attack the mole problem. I discovered that if you shot the moles in the ass, they would jump up, then fall down, stunned, before getting up and running away. That's how I spent my afternoons. Eventually, I got rid of the moles, although I don't know where they went.

On my first day home, I got a phone call from Bob Donovan.

"I got a lead on a couple cute women downtown," he said. "Get dressed and come with me."

It was a joke, of course. Donovan knew without a specific diagnosis that heart attack victims can fall into depression, and he was trying to cheer me up. But he'd hit the nail on the head. There I was, taking potshots at moles and feeling completely useless, a workaholic who couldn't work.

It was even worse than Donovan suspected. I seriously considered suicide, even working out the details. The best way, I decided, would be to start the car in the garage and let carbon monoxide do the job. Fortunately, I recognized the folly of this and went to see a psychiatrist instead. I've never been one of those who tries to deny mental or psychological issues because of the stigma associated with them. To me, if there's a problem, you identify it and fix it if you can.

So during this decade of heart problems and ensuing bouts of depression, I worked with a number of psychiatrists. I grew especially close to Dr. Leonard Egerman, who had been a cardiologist who himself suffered a heart attack. If anyone could empathize with me in my situation, it was Egerman. His advice to me was straightforward.

"Suicide," he said, "is the most selfish thing one can do."

I hadn't considered suicide a selfish act. Desperate, certainly, but not selfish. Then I thought about how my suicide would affect Judy and the kids, and I realized Egerman was right: Suicide wouldn't help anybody but me. With Egerman's guidance, I was able to put my suicidal thoughts in a broader, more appropriate context.

I viewed these visits as stages in a research project: I was trying to get a handle on my depression and, at the same time, explore the human condition more broadly. I really enjoy trying to figure out how we think, what goes through our heads. My attitude was, the more I know about myself, the more I'll know about other people. I think that insight made me a better manager.

Eventually, I felt well enough to return to work but I suffered bouts of depression — and continued treatment — for many years.

*   *   *   *   *

Act II — Heart Attack (Reprise)

The second heart attack came a year later — another Sunday morning in March. This attack wasn't as severe as the first one, but I had arteries full of plaque. Still, the doctors at this point weren't recommending bypass surgery; the state of the art was such that surgery may have been more risky than doing nothing. I returned to work more quickly — no mole hunts — only to find changed attitudes about me among some of my colleagues.

There were a couple young bucks who thought that if they eased me out, they could divvy up the spoils. "Now that you're injured," they would say, "you should give us a bunch of your work." Or, "You're endangering yourself by working so hard. Let us take over some of your responsibilities."

I resented it — hey, the corpse was still warm! Fortunately, I retained John Godfrey's strong support. I resolved to work even harder to show them how wrong they were and might well have worked myself to death if it hadn't been for Judy's determination to keep me ticking.

She knew that phoning me to suggest that I quit working for the day wouldn't do any good. So each day, at 5 or 5:30, she'd put some food out for the kids, drive to On-Line and hunt me down.

"Jack," she'd say, "it's time to come home."

Nothing stopped her. She even dragged me out of board meetings at times. Everyone at On-Line became familiar with the drill. As soon as they saw Judy, they would say, "See you tomorrow, Jack," and that would be that. She kept this up for about a year, and I was smart enough not to resist her.

* * * * *

Act III — Coronary Bypass Surgery

The next nine years passed without a major incident, although I was hospitalized briefly for checkups. But this was only the intermission, not the end of the drama.

In 1982, I began waking up in the middle of the night, this time feeling both pressure and pain. I wasn't breathing terribly well during the day, either. Our garage was in the basement, and I couldn't make it up the steps from the garage without stopping to catch my breath. Judy had taken to driving me to my appointments downtown because there was a good chance I wouldn't be able to walk from the parking garage to the office where I needed to go. All this was new and frightening. Donovan sent me to a specialist, Dr. Kennedy at St. Margaret Hospital in Pittsburgh.

"You're waking up in the middle of the night, you're supposed to be completely at rest, and you're having heart problems? That's very serious," Kennedy said. "You're definitely a candidate for bypass surgery. The state of the art in bypass surgery has really improved."

Kennedy made an appointment for me at the Cleveland Clinic, which at the time was considered a step ahead of Pittsburgh's hospitals in bypass surgery. I went to the clinic on a Friday for preliminary testing, with my heart catheterization scheduled for the following Monday. We spent the weekend at home. Periodically, I would run up and down the stairs, as if to show the world that I was fine, thank you, and didn't need any surgery. This was madness, and the catheterization confirmed it.

The blockages were so bad that they would not even let me out of bed, let alone out of the hospital. The surgeon was on vacation but returning Wednesday. I would be his first priority.

What an interesting experience that surgery was. I woke up briefly at one point in the procedure—can't say exactly what point it was — to hear two doctors conversing at the foot of my bed. One was saying:

"Let's try this. Let's take a chance."

My last thought before falling back to sleep was, "Holy shit, I'm a guinea pig!"

When I woke up fully, I saw nurses in the room and wanted to speak with them. Then I realized I still had a long, thick tube in my mouth that rendered speech impossible. So I grabbed one of the nurses by the arm and spelled out a message on her palm: "Will I live?"

"Well of course you will," she said.

The minute she spoke, I realized what a ridiculous question it was. What else would she say? "Bad news, pal. You're gonna croak any minute now."

I heard the voice of Wilcomb, my old boss at HoJo, echoing in my head:

"Roseman, you are a dumb shit."

*　*　*　*　*

Meanwhile, a drama of another sort was playing out in the waiting room. I had asked Ted Barnett, my best friend at the time, to sit with Judy.

"If something bad happens," I told him, "you'll be there to look out for her."

"I'll be there," he assured me.

Knowing Ted would be there comforted me. He was a short, barrel-chested guy, a high school football star in Bethesda who won a football scholarship to the University of Maryland. Ultimately, the coaches considered him too short for football at that level, so he joined the Air Force after graduation. There, Sgt. Barnett had persistent problems with one of his commanding officers, who had the endearing habit of calling Ted "you fucking Jew." It was the same prejudice — the same words, even — my father encountered a generation earlier in the Charlestown shipyards, and Ted handled it the same way Pa did: He challenged the officer to a fight.

The officer had a reputation as a skilled boxer, a Golden

Gloves champion, so Ted figured he'd better make his first punch a good one. It was, breaking the officer's jaw. Ted was court-martialed for attacking an officer. But when the judge heard testimony of the officer's anti-Semitism, he proposed a compromise. He would convict Ted — the rules required him to — but the Air Force would welcome Ted back as a sergeant the very next day. That's what happened. It might have been the briefest punishment in military history.

Ted was a great guy but a little emotional, and while I was on the operating table and in the recovery room, his emotions overwhelmed him. It was Judy who ended up comforting and reassuring him.

Cleveland Clinic at the time had well-structured, even rigid visitation policies. Family could not see their loved one the day of surgery, although they could call in at certain times for reports. Nurses were not to be disturbed at any time; if you didn't hear from them, you could assume everything was good.

Then, the day after surgery, all family reported to a 9 AM meeting when they were told what to expect over the next week, which was the typical length of stay back then for bypass patients. Finally, they would call the name of each patient and meet privately with the family for a status update.

When they called "Roseman," Judy approached a stern-faced nurse who told her, "We're not sure we can let him go."

Oh no. What now?

"He's just too much fun. He keeps asking the girls for dates. When we remind him that he's married, he says that you're understanding and will come along with us. He has us all in stitches, so we're not letting him off the floor."

No need to tell you how I spent my time once they removed

that cursed tube.

* * * * *

They finally let me go after about a week. I should have been overjoyed to be going home with a new lease on life, right? Instead, I kept thinking about how close to death I'd been — one little slip of the knife and it's Dearly Beloved — how I'd been living with half a heart, how I'd have to keep on living with half a heart. It really got to me. I could not stop crying. I learned later that crying spells are common among post-heart surgery patients; at the time, all I knew was that I was a mess. Judy had been staying at a hotel on the hospital grounds, and with the shape I was in, we decided to stay one more night in the hotel. I wanted to compose myself before I saw the kids.

Over the course of this decade of heart issues, I had plenty of time to think about my life, my death, and what I wanted from each. My damaged heart was a sword of Damocles hanging over my head. When you're in that situation, you want to make peace with the universe because you know that sword could fall any minute.

Some people in this situation embrace God; others curse him. I saw this in the hospitals when I encountered fellow heart attack victims. They would complain, "Why me, God, why me?" And I used to say, "Why not you? It's gotta be somebody. People *will* die from heart attacks. You just drew the lucky number. So it's meaningless to ask, 'Why me?'"

I saw a number of doctors prior to my surgery; several, including Dr. Kian Kooros, a renowned cardiologist at Passavant, suggested I retire or at least cut back significantly. That wasn't in the cards. I had to stay true to my values, and working hard and making a living for my family were at the top of the list. But I did resolve to spend more time with my kids. I determined that I would work as hard as ever six days a week, but I would reserve Sundays for my family. This might not seem like a big deal, one little day, but trust me. For a lifelong workaholic, it's a huge concession.

My heart problems, my sense that death was dangling over my head also pushed me to be even kinder to others. When I was a kid, I used to ask, "Why was I born?" To help others was the answer. Now, I would be even more helpful. Help more, judge less became my mantra.

I even developed a little routine to remind me of my resolve. My wristwatch in those days was not a fancy piece, just something off a department store shelf. But it did have plenty of bells and whistles, including an audible alarm. Each day, I set the alarm for midnight. When it sounded, it was a concrete reminder that I'd been lucky enough to live another day, lucky enough to be given still another day. Use it well, Yonkil.

* * * * *

I'd never had much luck with, or interest in, vacations — remember my leg injury on our honeymoon? I'd traveled enough for business, but that was always purposeful — no sightseeing, no kicking back, no tourist traps. After my heart attacks, though, I wanted to spend more time with Judy and the kids, and vacations were a great way to accomplish that. So we planned a family vacation to Puerto Rico — the kids were 15, 13 and 11.

Alas, the Roseman vacation hex continued. We reached Puerto Rico, seemingly in good shape. Then Judy developed some fairly serious respiratory symptoms and was diagnosed with pneumonia. She needed to fly home, but there weren't enough seats for all five of us. She flew back with Laura while I came on a later flight with Alan and Shari. Judy spent two weeks in the hospital. It was a memorable vacation — for all the wrong reasons.

Somebody seemed to be telling me, "Roseman, don't take vacations. You're not the vacation type." But there was still one place I wanted my children to experience — Israel. I wanted to re-enforce their identities as Jews, to let them experience a country where Jews did everything. I knew I had a shrinking window of opportunity for this: once the kids grew and started heading off to college, it was unlikely we would be able to experience Israel as a family. My precarious health also loomed large. My life was, literally, day to day. I couldn't defer this mission to a tomorrow that might not come.

So in 1979, when Laura was a senior in high school, I came up with a plan. During Christmas break for the kids, we would combine a family vacation in Israel with business meetings I had in London. Israel first, then London. On paper, it looked great. In real life, I can assure you National Lampoon and the Griswolds never had a vacation like this.

The first problem was luggage — we were overwhelmed with it. We needed cold-weather clothing for London with the complete business mufti for me. But for Israel, we needed lighter, less formal clothing. The result — 10 overstuffed pieces of luggage that we couldn't fit into a conventional car or cab. On-Line Systems came to the rescue by sending a truck that could accommodate all 10 pieces.

We were to fly from New York to the Netherlands via KLM, then change planes at Schiphol Airport for the final leg to Israel. Not a single segment of that itinerary went smoothly. When we reached the terminal at New York and unloaded all our luggage, we were advised that we would need to proceed to a second terminal for luggage check-in and boarding. So we *schlepped* the luggage out, hailed two cabs for the baggage and us and proceeded to the second terminal. Because our ultimate destination was Israel, security insisted on checking every item in every piece of luggage, including our carry-ons. As you can imagine, this whole process took hours.

We finally reached Schiphol and were preparing to change planes when the airline popped another surprise on us: our seats on the connecting flight already were occupied, and they could not honor our tickets. We were faced with the prospect of being stranded at the airport with 10 pieces of luggage and no tickets out. Fortunately, I knew some people in Amsterdam, including an attorney who I thought could help us. I phoned him. Before long, the airline told us that we would be more than welcome on their plane. Finally, we were en route to Israel.

We spent eight days in Israel, eight days that were magical and awe inspiring. To see Jews everywhere—the cab drivers were Jewish, the soldiers were Jewish, the police were Jewish, the trash collectors were Jewish — brought me, and I think the rest of my family, a new level of contentment and confidence. No cause for paranoia here, no reason to speculate on how others regarded us. We felt home, perhaps closer as a family than we'd ever been.

To a certain extent, that feeling persists to this day, although the intensity of the experience faded a bit when our return trip turned out to be one more nightmare.

We were scheduled to fly to London via Rome. Unbeknownst to us, the time of our connecting flight was changed, and we missed it. So we were stranded overnight in Rome, which doesn't sound like a bad thing. Except this night was New Year's Eve, and the hotel where the airline put us up was so busy with New Year's Eve parties that they couldn't be bothered with us. We had to plead with them for a plate of spaghetti so the five of us could eat.

Next morning, when we arrived at the airport, we realized our passports were back at the hotel. The passports reached the airport just in time, and we flew to London only to find that the baggage handlers at Heathrow were not particularly keen on having to work New Year's Day. They dawdled. We waited several hours in a freezing room with cement walls before we could collect our luggage.

It was as stressful a trip as could be, and I paid the price for it. When we arrived at our hotel, I felt significant chest pain. We found a doctor, and while he examined me, Judy trundled the kids up in a cab, slipped the driver some notes and said: "Show them London." They saw more of it than I did. I spent the entire time in London in bed, per doctor's orders, missing all my meetings.

When I felt well enough to fly, we ordered tickets for the flight, reminding the airline how important it was for the five of us to be seated together. They scattered us all over the plane, but even that wasn't the end of our woes. We arrived at JFK only to learn that our flight to Pittsburgh had been canceled, so we needed another two-cab caravan to get us to Newark and a flight home, the final insult on the Trip From Hell.

*   *   *   *   *

We made it safely home. My pain disappeared, and I was able to distill the pleasures from the chaos our vacation became.

As it did every night, my wristwatch alarm went off at midnight. Before turning in, I spent a few minutes appreciating the day on earth I'd been granted, a few minutes anticipating the day about to begin.

12. PERSON OF INTEREST

When I returned to work following my second heart attack, one of my major emphases was servicing a contract we had won from the U.S. Department of Health, Education, and Welfare — we were helping HEW with the research and automation of its Guaranteed Student Loan Monitoring System. The contract was worth $7.5 million over the life of the deal, so it was a major piece of business that took me to Washington regularly, although the bulk of the actual work was done in our San Francisco office.

Our San Francisco folks worked long hours with their HEW counterparts, often until 9 or 10 at night. Afterwards, they would repair to a restaurant for a late dinner — On-Line always picked up the check. When I was reviewing these dinner receipts, I found some ranging up to $500, including $100 bottles of wine. San Francisco can be an expensive city, of course, and if I'd seen one or two $500 receipts, I probably would have let them pass. But there were numerous receipts in the $500 range, and that simply was too much to be lavishing on a public-sector client.

I sent a memo to our staff reminding them that any meals we provided for HEW employees had to be consistent with government rules on gifts, and that in all cases, the prices for meals we provide must be "reasonable." That, I thought, takes care of that.

In the course of my time in Washington, I made another important discovery: the head of the DC office, a man named Harry Z — I don't want to identify him for reasons that will become obvious — was planning to leave On-Line and take some of our customers with him. Worse, he was writing his business plan on our computers. I was furious, angrier than I might otherwise have been because I really liked Harry. When I confronted Harry with the incontrovertible evidence, my rage boiled over.

"You're fired," I said. "I don't ever wanna see you again. And if I do see you again, I'll kill you."

It was hyperbole, of course, just my anger talking, but those few ill-chosen words had major consequences — for Roseman and On-Line.

*   *   *   *   *

I was home one Sunday, not too long after firing Harry Z, when the doorbell rang. I opened the door to the chief of police of Ross Township. This was not terribly alarming because I knew the chief. In fact, his daughter was my secretary at On-Line, although I didn't know of the relationship when I hired her.

I invited him in.

"Do you know a man named Harry Z?" he asked.

"I not only know him, I just fired his ass. And if I ever see him again, I'll kill him."

The chief looked pained.

"Don't say that," he cautioned. Then he explained why he'd come to see me.

Mike DeJohn, On-Line's sales manager and a decorated former Green Beret, had been found shot to death in his garage. As soon as Mike's wife, Jill, reported the murder, the police began an investigation. At some point early in the investigation, my good friend Harry Z called the police and pointed out how amazing it was that I had threatened to kill him, and now Mike DeJohn, another On-Line employee, had died *in exactly the same way I swore I'd kill Harry!* Could that really be a coincidence?

Thanks to my intemperate words to Harry, I was now a person of interest in the murder of a man I liked and respected very much.

But the repercussions didn't end there. John Godfrey and I learned that On-Line was the subject of a federal investigation into the awarding of On-Line's contracts with HEW and the U.S. Senate. The feds had been informed that we had provided money under the table to get those contracts, and that I had fired the head of the DC office because he refused to participate in such illegalities. Harry Z strikes again!

I met with the lead investigator, who showed me a wad of familiar-looking receipts from San Francisco restaurants.

"Don't you think these bills are a little outrageous?" he said.

"Yes, but let me show you a memo that I sent after I saw these."

He read my memo impassively.

"You just say in here to be reasonable. Reasonable prices."

"What do you consider reasonable prices?

"It's not for me to say, but clearly $500 is not reasonable."

"I didn't know what the exact figure should be, so I said 'reasonable.' I followed the rules."

"You should have put down a certain amount. I don't know what that amount is — that's for you to figure out, not me."

It wasn't enough that I was a person of interest in a murder. Now, I also was a person of interest in a federal kickbacks investigation.

* * * * *

It didn't take long for the police to determine that it wasn't an intruder or irate boss who murdered Mike. His wife, Jill, had a conviction for extortion on her record. The police questioned her sister, who disclosed that Jill had once proposed that they kill their father to collect their inheritance early. Then they found, through subpoenas of Jill's bank records, that she had run up huge debts. The last piece of the puzzle: Mike had a $201,000 insurance policy that named Jill the beneficiary.

The crazy thing about this is that, when we learned of the shooting, Judy actually visited Jill at the DeJohn home to see if she could help and offer general support. Jill was one cool customer, playing the part of the grieving widow to a T.

Jill went to trial in 1976. The judge wouldn't allow testimony about her proposed plot to kill her father — it was too prejudicial — but even that didn't help Jill. She was convicted of third-degree murder — a strange charge, I thought, given that this murder was well planned and that there was no passion involved. It seemed like a textbook case of murder in the first degree. Be that as it may, the Pennsylvania Supreme Court in 1980 ruled that the police subpoenas were illegal and threw out Jill's conviction. In 1982, she was retried, again convicted of third-degree murder and sentenced to 8-1/2-to-20 years in prison.

*   *   *   *   *

My troubles in Washington didn't vanish so easily.

The investigation dragged on for about a year. The case made national headlines, including a big story in the *Wall Street Journal*. Still another newspaper article speculated that the investigations of On-Line Systems and the murder of Mike DeJohn would lead directly to the Mafia. John and I emphasized our innocence each time we spoke with a reporter, for all the good that did us. This thing was hurting my heart — literally — and it wasn't doing our business any good, either, particularly in the government sector. Who wants to sign a contract with a company that's under federal investigation?

Finally, a grand jury was empaneled. I traveled to Washington with On-Line's attorney, Bill Newlin of the Pittsburgh firm Buchanan Ingersoll, to see the U.S. attorney.

"I understand you've called a grand jury," I said. "I would like to be called to testify. I'm tired of having all these rumors going around, so let me talk to the grand jury. And let me tell you something. When I'm through testifying, either Jack Roseman or Harry Z better wind up in jail because one of them is lying."

Newlin was practically strangling me to shut me up, but I was on a roll. That's how sure I was that I was innocent. The U.S. attorney seemed amused . . . and not unsympathetic.

"Let Jack talk," he said. "I don't blame him for feeling the way he does."

I *was* called to testify, and it was quite an experience. The questions they asked me all were legitimate, yet they were slanted in such a way that it appeared On-Line's guilt was assumed.

"I can see you've come to the conclusion that we're guilty," I told the grand jury, "but let me tell you my side of it."

I was on the stand for about an hour, and it was grueling. Then one of the jurors, a forbidding-looking African-American, called for a caucus. I was sure my goose was cooked. I later learned this juror understood how demanding the questioning was for a guy with heart problems — the U.S. attorney had told them about my health issues — and the juror wanted to give me a chance to catch my breath and relax. Just shows once again that you never should prejudge or pigeonhole people.

I'm not sure how effective my testimony was, but in the end, the grand jury didn't hand up any indictments. Ordinarily when that happens, the U.S attorney issues a statement citing "insufficient evidence." In our case, he not only cited insufficient evidence, but he also took pains to note that On-Line had been victimized by unfavorable media coverage that was unfair because no crime had been committed.

The investigation was a tough time for us, and it left me with mixed feelings. I was happy to be exonerated, of course, and gratified by the number of customers who sent us letters of support. We even got one from the president of the American Bankers Association. On the other hand, I was miffed that Harry Z did not go to jail, did not, as far as I could tell, suffer any punishment for falsely impugning us. In this regard, justice was not served.

*   *   *   *   *

Toward the end of the '70s, there was talk among some of On-Line's most important shareholders, including the Ladenburg Thalmann group, that it might be an appropriate time to sell the company. Our stock had split several times; on paper, On-Line's shareholders, particularly those who got in on the ground floor, were a lot wealthier as a result of their On-Line investments. However, virtually all of them had held their shares and hadn't realized an actual penny of profit yet.

I wasn't particularly keen on selling. John and I had built On-Line into an international player, a company with annual revenue of about $35 million, a profit margin that often reached 15 percent and about 500 employees. For many shareholders, the sale of On-line would mean a huge financial windfall. For Jack Roseman, it would mean a sizable payday, to be sure, but I would miss the work. I enjoyed fighting the battles, especially high-level, high-stake battles. And if I didn't have On-Line, what would I do for a living?

Yet I knew selling was the right thing for the people who had supported us for nearly a decade, so I couldn't bring myself to oppose it. John and I insisted on one condition: Any purchaser would have to agree to maintain operations in Pittsburgh. We wanted to assure that as many On-Line employees as possible could maintain their positions with the purchasing company without enduring the dislocations of moving to another headquarters city.

I don't know it for sure, but I think Ladenburg Thalmann put out feelers that the company was for sale, for we soon had a couple suitors. The first potential buyers we met were the senior executives of a company called ADP, which had data processing centers all over the United States and eventually would become a global player. We met with the company founder, Henry Taub, who wouldn't agree to keep a company presence in Pittsburgh, so we quickly nixed that deal.

The next prospective purchaser was more serious. United Telecommunications, a forerunner of today's Sprint, had grown large and prosperous by gobbling up local phone companies. They had a time-sharing unit, but its reach was exclusively domestic. On-Line's operations abroad appealed to them. Once United Telecom agreed to keep On-Line in Pittsburgh, the game was on.

John decided to handle the negotiations himself — a mistake, I think, given the vast experience of Ladenburg Thalmann in these kinds of matters. He agreed to a price of

$23.94 per share, payable in United Telecom stock, which I thought was a lowball offer. And I had more than a passing interest in the sales price. For John and others who had founders' shares that they'd purchased for pennies, the sale price wasn't all that significant. Didn't matter whether the sale price-per-share was $20 or $25. They were going to realize huge gains and become millionaires many times over. For those of us who had purchased our shares or options at market rates, the difference of a dollar or two in the sale price-per-share could be enormous.

I decided to do a little negotiating of my own. I went to Kansas City, where United Telecom was headquartered, to meet with their executive vice president and another executive — my counterpart, actually, who headed their time-sharing unit. Over dinner, I spoke bluntly.

"You should know that I'm opposed to this sale," I told them.

"Why is that?"

"I think you're getting away with murder. On-Line is worth more than what you've offered for it."

While the executive vice president was taking this in, his colleague asked him: "Should we give them the other offer we've prepared?" This was not exactly an effective negotiating ploy. With one sentence, he had confirmed my suspicion that their offer was lowball, and that there was a better price to be had.

I worked on them the rest of the evening and walked away with an offer that was about 10 percent higher than the original bid. I returned to On-Line the next day feeling pretty satisfied with myself. But when I shared the good news with John, he was less than pleased.

"I shook hands at the lower price," he said. "I have to honor my word."

Still, I wasn't ready to accept it. I phoned Finkel, our board member, who was unequivocal in his support for John's position.

"Once you shake hands," Finkel said, "you got a deal."

So we accepted the lowball offer, and my clever bargaining went for naught.

The deal was completed in November 1979. I didn't expect United Telecom to carry John and me very long. Indeed, they'd already picked out an executive to move into John's office and kept hounding John to get his butt out of there so they could reallocate his space. John obliged them after a few weeks. But they wanted me to stay on and help them with next year's business plan, even offering me a three-year contract if I would do so.

I met with an executive named Lorenzo who was heading up the budgeting process. Lorenzo asked me for my sales projections for the next year. I suggested he build in a modest increase, say $1 million or $2 million more than the current year's revenue. I haggled with Lorenzo over the course of an afternoon, but he wouldn't accept my figures.

"This is ridiculous," I said. "Just tell me what numbers you want, and I'll fill them in."

"Oh no. The numbers have to be yours."

"But you keep rejecting my projections."

"That's because you're sandbagging me."

"Lorenzo, I won't be with your company long. There's no reason for me to sandbag you."

"Then give me better numbers."

By the time we ended, the modest gain I'd suggested had ballooned into the $5 million increase that Lorenzo wanted, a completely unrealistic revenue projection. Lorenzo's eyes sparkled.

"And that's how I earn my money!" he said in triumph.

It was a complete charade and altogether typical of corporate bureaucracies — impose what you want and make it appear that it emanated from your employees. I responded as evenly as I could.

"Let me suggest that you don't spend that $5 million until you see it."

*   *   *   *   *

I left the company not too long after John's departure. The timing of On-Line's sale, and our departure from United Telecom, was exquisite. The advent of personal computers was about to render time-sharing obsolete. Every company in that space would disappear or morph into something dramatically different. Lorenzo's $5 million projected revenue bump was about to go up in smoke.

I'd like to tell you that our timely exit was the result of careful planning and stunning insight, but it was luck. And I say that as a veteran entrepreneur who knows how important it is to have all the skills and to work them round the clock. You need those attributes, but you can't dismiss luck, and fortune favored us this time. Even though we accepted United Telecom's inadequate offer, I walked away with $1 million. I don't know exactly how much John realized, but I'm guessing it was in the $3 million-plus range.

He retired and bought a farm north of Pittsburgh. We still got together from time to time. Once, over coffee, his banter turned serious. John didn't show his emotions very often, and I could tell he was about to speak from the heart.

"If ever you need money," he said, "I want you to know I'm there."

"I don't need money."

"But if you ever do, I'll be there."

I appreciated that this was his way of apologizing for botching the sale negotiations and costing me and other shareholders significant profits — in my case, about $200,000. But I wasn't angry with John. He had an enormous influence on my career. In bringing me to On-Line, he helped me get as close to my most cherished professional goal as I ever would come. He died several years ago, and I miss him to this day.

13. OF HEARTS, HORSES & BEER CANS

The sale of On-Line Systems was timely; the era of computer time-sharing was just about over. With the advent of personal computers, businesses could acquire all the hardware and software they needed relatively inexpensively, and they were developing the requisite in-house expertise to network and troubleshoot their computers. In a decade, time-sharing had gone from darling to dinosaur.

Ahhh, but what would you do with your computers once you had them? Heretofore, computers had been used for data processing — in many cases sophisticated data processing, to be sure — and analysis. Now, the business world was hungry for applications.

I was pondering where I could plug in when I was approached with a business proposal involving just such an application. The American Heart Association (AHA) had pioneered technology that enabled computerized instruction of cardiopulmonary resuscitation (CPR). Before this advance, CPR students worked on mannequins as a nurse/instructor stood by and supervised. Students first placed their fingers on the mannequin's throat to detect a pulse. They would breathe into the mannequin's mouth, to give the victim some air, and then compress the chest. More often than not, this routine of chest compressions and air was all there was to it. It wasn't demanding, and students got their certifications without many problems or delays.

(By the way, did you know that almost all the mannequins used in CPR instruction bear the same face? Towards the end of the 19th century, a young French woman, said to have been disappointed in love, threw herself in the Seine and drowned. The morgue director was so captivated by the face of "L'Inconnue de la Seine" — "The Unknown Woman of the Seine" — that he made a mold of it. That mold became the basis for death masks that sold like crazy throughout Europe. Among the proud owners of a death mask was Asmund Laerdal, a Norwegian industrialist who operated a toy-making factory. According to *Pitt Med* magazine, in 1960, the University of Pittsburgh's Dr. Peter Safar, a CPR pioneer, asked Laerdal to create a mannequin for this new technique. Laerdal agreed and used the death mask for his mannequins' faces. The unfortunate woman, who became the post-mortem rock star of CPR, now is known as "Resusci Anne." The story of her death may be apocryphal, but Resusci Anne remains the gold standard of mannequins.)

The American Heart Association set out to improve the system. They still used Resusci Anne, but they equipped her with about 17 sensors and connected her to a computer that could speak, in a woman's voice, to students working on Anne. When students, learning the location of the pulse, probed for it, they actually could feel it; if they didn't, they knew they had to reposition their fingers.

Best of all, the computer was programmed to determine just the right amount of compression needed. If you didn't press hard enough, the computer would tell you. If you pressed too hard, the computer would politely suggest that you just broke the victim's rib please try again. Human instructors still might be standing by, but there no longer would be a real need for them.

While AHA owned the technology, it needed a partner to commercialize it. For that, it tapped a group that included an emergency room physician named Danny Cassidy, who was affiliated with the association, and two engineering professors from the University of Pittsburgh who worked with AHA and Cassidy. The professors asked me to review the business plan they'd developed and, if I liked it, to join them as CEO.

The idea intrigued me. As a mathematician, I liked the precision of the technology. There would be no guesswork about the proper amount of pressure. Students would learn exactly what pressure to apply, making them more effective in CPR. That, of course, could save lives. AHA had a prototype at Pitt — I liked what I saw of it. Moreover, the emerging relationship had a certain poetry: Here's Roseman, he of the two heart attacks and coronary bypass surgery, working for healthy hearts across the land.

I whipped the business plan into shape, and our new company, which we called Actronics, was off and running. In retrospect, it's clear my due diligence wasn't as thorough as it should have been. To this day, when somebody solicits my support for a new venture, I ask several key questions: Do you have any proof that the market will be receptive? Who are your customers? Why would they buy this product? What would they be willing to pay for it? I pursued these questions thoroughly with AHA; they reassured me each time. They were convinced doctors and hospitals would be lining up to buy this technology, and I believed them.

I should have known better, but this one was from the heart.

* * * * *

Judy worked with the prototype at Pitt and was as fascinated by it as I was. By this time, she already had her master's degree in computer science from Pitt as well as her teaching certificate in math from Duquesne University. Completing her education had become more urgent for her; with my health a question mark, she never knew when she might need to go to work to support our family.

School, in her view, was a necessity, yet she found it therapeutic as well. As we were putting the finishing touches on the Actronics business structure, she asked if the company had a position for her. Danny loved the idea, but I was wary. I had seen spouses work in the same office. Usually, their relationship, the company or both suffered. Yet she had valuable expertise, and no one needed to remind me how smart and diligent she is.

"You can join us," I said, "but don't hang any pictures because you're not staying around long."

She hung pictures all right, and she stayed at Actronics for the entire five years I was there, working 60-hour weeks and never complaining. I did insist on certain conditions. She would report to Danny, the chairman, rather than Jack, the CEO. She never could make more than her starting salary of $25,000, so I couldn't be accused of nepotism in showering her with raises. And we would travel in different cars, so that if one of us needed to see a client, for example, the other could still go home and tend to affairs there. We both became quite committed to Actronics and its goals. You could see it in the license plates of our cars. Mine was, and still is, ACTRON. Judy's was, and still is, INOCPR. In fact, when AHA revised its CPR instructions, as they did every four years or so, Judy wrote scripts for the videos.

*   *   *   *   *

Actronics introduced several other computerized teaching programs, including Advanced Cardiac Life Support (ACLS). Yet for all our innovation and hard work, the company never was as successful as we projected. We encountered several unanticipated obstacles. Price was one. The research of Danny and my other partners indicated that hospitals and other customers would be willing to pay up to

$5,000 for a system, so that's the figure we built into our business plan. But as we got more deeply into operations, we found that we couldn't make a profit unless we sold our systems for $25,000, a price the market would not be willing to bear.

Still another issue was that students could not waltz through training as quickly as they would have liked. If you were off in your compressions by just a little, the computer would not certify you. You had to repeat the process — as many times as it took to get it right. This was a particular problem for hospitals, where doctors weren't terribly interested in training that took up too much of their time. Hospitals were accustomed to giving something akin to "drive-by" training and rubber-stamping certificates.

Moreover, most hospitals used nurses as their CPR trainers, and nurses were understandably reluctant to advise doctors — who would become their supervisors again in a few minutes — that their oafishness had broken the rib of poor little Resusci Anne.

We got a cold dose of reality when we offered a California health system a free trial. The organization operated many hospitals and medical offices, so this could have been our big breakthrough.

"Give our system a try for a month," I told them. "I know you'll be so impressed you'll buy a bunch of them."

A month later, they called and asked us to remove the system.

"You're not happy with it?"

They definitely were not happy with it, and they told me why.

"You don't understand the way we teach CPR here," they said. "We're like a mass marketer of CPR training. Doctors want their certificates in a hurry. Your system holds us up."

We had one or two hospitals that really liked it because those institutions were run by perfectionists. Firefighters, as well, appreciated the accuracy of the Actronics system. Our best customer by far was the United States Marine Corps, which bought our systems for many of their bases. Unlike others, they *wanted* a tough system, they *wanted* a precise system. But they were one of a handful of exceptions.

Judy got a first-hand glimpse of how hospitals were confirming that doctors knew basic CPR — a prerequisite for ACLS certification — during a training/certification session at Pitt for emergency room physicians; Judy participated as an observer. She watched as the doctors strolled in, worked briefly on Resusci Anne and got their compressions all wrong; many failed to check for a pulse. Yet the instructor presented each of them with a certification card.

Judy watched in agony for a while before she couldn't stay silent any longer.

"You know how important CPR is," Judy said. "You know these doctors don't have it right, but you're certifying them anyway."

"Their jobs depend on it," the instructor said.

Their jobs depend on it? What about the lives that might depend on proper administration of CPR? That's what Judy was thinking, but she said nothing. What was the point?

* * * * *

Actronics never penetrated the hospital market to the degree we needed for comfortable profitability.

Truth be told, I have a different view of our system today

than I did when I was with Actronics. I don't know if the system had to be *that* tough. Could it have been as effective with a tolerance of, say, 10 percent or 20 percent? AHA and the Red Cross — the only two CPR certifying agencies at the time — wouldn't budge from the exacting standard. I don't think that degree of accuracy turned out to be that critical.

But that's second-guessing. The fact of the matter was that Actronics' board of directors was not entirely pleased with my performance, although I don't want to suggest there was any rancor. It simply was time for new leadership, perhaps a team that could present the system in compelling new ways. In 1987, I resigned and sold my Actronics shares privately to one of our board members.

I suggested to the board that they look for a marketing dynamo who could convey the advantages of the system more persuasively than we had. Instead, the board promoted our chief financial officer to succeed me — and another finance guy to succeed him. None of that helped much, and Actronics eventually was sold to the Norwegian company that introduced Resusci Anne. So far as I know, she's still on the job.

*   *   *   *   *

I've always loved animals, although as a kid from the ghetto, I'd had little access to animals except our family dog, and I always had a taste for gambling. I think that stemmed from my mother's passion for bingo and penny-ante poker. At the time, my child's mind magnified the risks. Put love of animals and gambling together and you get . . . horse racing.

In the '70s and '80s, legal gambling options were pretty limited. You could go to Las Vegas (Atlantic City came along later), or you could go to the racetrack. When we lived in Maryland, I occasionally went to Rosecroft, a Standardbred (harness racing) track right off the beltway. I would go to the track after work, around 7 or 8 in the evening, have a hot dog, watch horses and make a couple bets. I lost, mostly, but the thrill of watching beautiful animals perform and pitting my skills against those of other bettors was considerable.

After we moved to Pittsburgh, I discovered that Chuck Daly, an ex-Marine whom John Godfrey and I hired as chief financial officer for On-Line Systems, enjoyed racing as much as I did. Judy and I often went with Chuck and his wife to The Meadows, a harness track about 25 miles southwest of town. Judy, I must say, liked racing, though not nearly as much as I did, but she indulged me. Sometimes we even made a weekend of it, taking in the Friday and Saturday cards and staying overnight at the Holiday Inn just down the road from The Meadows.

That might have been the extent of my involvement, except for a chance encounter at a beer can show. The caterers of the event were the family of Dean Zaimes, a trainer and driver at The Meadows. I had seen Dean drive many times at the track, so when his father suggested to Judy that Dean might be willing to partner with me in a horse, I was very interested. When I met with Dean, he offered to buy a horse named Popcorn Kid that Dean's father and I would own. I accepted his offer and, like that, I was a horseman.

People become horse owners for two reasons — the fun of watching their horses race and the chance to make a profit. The first part is easy, but making a profit? Often, that's unattainable simply because income may not offset expenses. On the expense side, your trainer—Dean Zaimes, in my case — charges you a daily fee. Plus you have food, veterinary care and medicine. In addition, your trainer and your driver — the harness racing equivalent of jockey — each takes 5 percent of any purse money your horse wins. At the time, those expenses added up to about $12,000 per year. So if your horse didn't earn at least $12,000, you were in the hole. Many owners never dig out of that hole and fade from the business.

Popcorn Kid earned more than $12,000, so I made money and thought, this game is easy. It turned out to be not so easy, but Judy, Chuck, his wife El and I had a ball. We frequently watched the races from the 2:00 Club, a trackside restaurant for horse owners. I became close with Mary Wohlmuth, the club's manager, and got to know other horsemen and horsewomen. Before long, I was part of the racing community at The Meadows. We even became partners in horses with people we met at the 2:00 Club.

Over the years, I had other horses with Zaimes and a few other trainers, including Dave Dempster and the Snyder brothers, Dane and Doug. I was a hands-on manager in my other entrepreneurial ventures, but in harness racing, I knew I never could accumulate the knowledge my trainers had absorbed by working in the business all their lives. So I generally let them call the shots. I did insist that they run a clean business — no illegal medications to make my horses run faster.

There were times when I thought a trainer wasn't working out for us and I needed to move our horses to a different trainer. In short, I needed to fire the trainer, and I couldn't bring myself to do it. I'd hired and fired hundreds of people, but the relationships in racing are so intensely personal that changing trainers is more like executing a friend.

Once, when I was in this situation and dithering about it, Alan bailed me out. He went to the track, took our best horse from the trainer we were firing and led the horse to our new trainer. It was a tribute to Alan's persuasiveness and charm that everybody involved in the equation remained friends.

* * * * *

A would-be owner can acquire a horse in a number of ways. You can purchase a horse, solely or in partnership, from its current owner. You can buy a horse at auction. You can claim a horse out of certain races. If, for example, the race features $10,000 claiming horses, every horse in that race can be purchased on the spot for $10,000. You drop your name in the claims box, write a certified check for $10,000 plus taxes, and the horse is yours at the end of the race.

But the most interesting and exciting way to get a horse is to breed one. If you own a mare, you can buy a breeding to a commercial stallion. When the mare gives birth, the foal is yours to raise, train and race. Or you can sell the foal if you choose. Stud fees in Thoroughbred racing can be outrageous — $300,000 or more for a top stallion. In the Standardbred game, fees are more affordable, so many owners like to go the breeding route.

Chuck and I bought a mare named Happy Evelyn from Jeff Mallet, a Pittsburgh kid who had trained and raced a champion named Dragon's Lair. The purchase price was $25,000, but she was well bred — her sire was a champion named Most Happy Fella — and we had high hopes for her. Dean Zaimes trained and drove Happy Evelyn. The first time she raced for us, Zaimes told us not to expect miracles.

"She hasn't raced in a long time, so I'm not gonna push her," Zaimes said.

Chuck and I left work early to see Happy Evelyn race. Outside the track, we bought a tip sheet — some so-called expert's picks for each race — and we noticed that Happy Evelyn was the tipster's "Best Bet" of the day. On the one hand, we had Zaimes' advice not to bet on Happy Evelyn. On the other hand, some tipster was calling her a sure thing. The rational choice would have been to keep our hands in our pockets, but we let our emotions get in the way. Chuck and I made substantial bets on Happy Evelyn. Zaimes, true to his word, didn't push her, and she finished last. I looked at Chuck, he looked at me, and we cracked up laughing. We knew we had succumbed to emotion, and we knew we would continue to do so as long as we were in this game.

It was clear before long that Happy Evelyn would lose us a ton of money if we kept racing her. But with her outstanding pedigree, we wondered if we should breed her and produce a young horse for us. We knew nothing about breeding, so we went to the most authoritative source we could find— Delvin Miller, the founder of The Meadows and the most respected, revered man in harness racing. He was generous with his time and advice. Over drinks at the 2:00 Club, we explained our situation.

"You really ought to breed her to Warm Breeze," Delvin said. "He's standing at Hanover Shoe Farms. That's what I would do if that were my mare."

The service fee for Warm Breeze was $3,000 — not unreasonable—so we took Delvin's advice and bred Happy Evelyn to Warm Breeze. In the old days of racing, the sire and dam actually would breed, but when you have two large, valuable animals thrashing around, you have the real potential for injury. That's why today, most of the breeding is done through artificial insemination. I took Judy and all the kids to Hanover Shoe Farms, which is in central Pennsylvania, not far from Gettysburg. Hanover was kind enough to allow us to watch the procedure they used to "collect" semen from their stallions. They bring in a mare in heat to excite the stallion. Then, the stud mounts a wooden "horse" covered with fur. A veterinarian collects the ejaculate in a special receptacle.

Though the industry has refined the collection process quite a bit since then — they now freeze semen and ship it all over the world — the basics haven't changed. It was a jaw-dropping experience for the Rosemans. We now understood the meaning of the expression "hung like a horse."

Happy Evelyn gave birth to a healthy foal that we named Adam Hadem, a play on the phrase A Dam Had Him. Then someone suggested we change his name to Actron, to honor Actronics. We did, and he became our prized racehorse. He raced 270 times in his career and won nearly $160,000 in purses.

Actron was a beloved pet to me, not some cold financial asset to be traded or liquidated when the market dictated. I visited him frequently, usually taking a three-pound bag of carrots with me. Once when I came to see him, his trainer at the time, Dane Snyder, said Actron was off his feed. I went into his stall, nuzzled him and fed him a carrot. Then a second carrot. Then another. In a flash, the bag was gone. I had been able to reassure him, and he was back on top of his game.

* * * * *

Through Mary Wohlmuth and the folks at the 2:00 Club, I became friendly with officials of the Meadows Standardbred Owners Association, which represents horse owners and trainers in their dealings with the track. Management owns the track, and it owns the racing dates, which are awarded by the state. But it doesn't own the horses. And if management wants horses to compete at its track, it needs to contract with the owners of those horses. The contract, like most management-labor contracts, is quite lengthy and detailed, specifying such items as the amount of purses and the percent of handle that goes to horse owners. Negotiations can be difficult and intense. A few years before I started frequenting The Meadows, a walkout by horsemen cost the track many race dates and nearly became violent.

I became vice president of the MSOA and was part of the team negotiating a new contract with Ladbroke, the owner of the track. We reached agreement on a deal that everyone could live with, and it led to management-labor accord that persists to this day.

My fervor for horse ownership cooled somewhat thanks to our relationship with a couple, Herb and Betty, who were partners with us in a horse. We met them at the 2:00 Club, liked them, and bought a horse with them named Tenacious Way. He turned out to be a promising young trotter who was eligible for a big stake race in the state of New York. As luck would have it, he wasn't completely sound a few days before the race, and our veterinarian recommended that we not enter him lest he cause himself real damage. Herb and Betty wanted to race him — they dearly wanted to compete in a major stake — but I refused to permit it.

"This is a chance to win big," Betty said.

"The horse's health means more to me than the money," I countered.

She looked at me with disgust.

"I always knew you were small minded," she said.

That was the end of our partnership. Herb and Betty transferred their ownership share to the horse's trainer. Tenacious Way earned more than $85,000 over nine years of racing, although we lost him to a claim late in his career. Judy, Chuck and I owned about a dozen horses over 15 years and loved most of our experiences as owners. But the incident with Herb and Betty left a bad taste in my mouth. I still watch the races on cable, but I no longer have the ownership bug.

* * * * *

Both Actronics and Actron were gone from my life — when Actron's racing days were over, we found a good home for him where he could enjoy a comfortable retirement. In this period of taking stock, it was time to bid farewell to yet another old friend.

I'd been collecting and trading beer cans for the better part of 30 years, but like everything else, beer cans weren't what they used to be. Cans with unique, memorable designs had given way to standard-issue, cookie-cutter units. Very few of them were worth anything; very few of them would appreciate in value.

I had been thinning my collection bit by bit, including a particularly valuable piece — an Iron City original from the 1930s. What made this can so special were the written instructions on its face on how to use a beer can opener. That shows you how novel beer can openers were in that era. I got a call from a collector who must have seen the Iron City can when I had it on display at a show.

"How much do you want for it?" he asked.

"It's $900. And if you offer me $899.99, you ain't getting it. We can negotiate over any other can, but this price is non-negotiable."

He thought about it for a while, then came to the house a week or two later and bought the can for $900.

This story has sort of a sad postscript. About six months later, I bumped into the purchaser at a beer can show. He told me he'd been laid off and really was struggling. I offered to buy back the Iron City can at the original price as a way of helping him, but he declined. Never saw him or the Iron City can again.

I divested some beer cans by donating them to WQED, the PBS television station in Pittsburgh, for their fund-raising auctions. For those events, viewers donated furniture, antiques, paintings and other goods that WQED auctioned on air. Judy and I bought some paintings and antiques through their auctions — we still have some of the pieces. It was a fun way to help a local nonprofit, and I enjoyed bidding and watching the auction to see if my bids would hold up. I donated many cases of beer cans; WQED auctioned them as a single lot that brought $700.

That still left me with about 2,500 cans. At a number of shows, I let it be known that I might be willing to entertain offers for the entire collection. Sure enough, I got a call from a collector in Ohio who said he might be interested. It was a six-hour drive for him, he said, but he was willing to make the trip.

I figured the collection probably was worth around $2,000. But here's what my experience as an entrepreneur told me: If my prospect was willing to drive for 12 hours round trip to inspect my collection, he would be loathe to go home empty handed. *(Yonkil, know your customer.)* So I set the price at $2,500. I understand this was not high finance. I fully appreciate that the difference between $2,000 and $2,500 is negligible in the scheme of things. But if you think that extra $500 should have been insignificant to me, then you don't know Jack. The art of the deal, remaining true to your principles—these mean everything.

When he arrived, he asked for 30 minutes alone to inspect

the cans. Finally, he was ready to deal.

"How much?"

"I'm asking $2,500."

"Whoa. That's really high."

"That's what it's worth to me. If you don't want it, fine. We'll still be friends."

When he drove back to Ohio, he was 2,500 beer cans richer.

* * * * *

When I left Actronics, I was 56 years old with no immediate business prospects, no companies I was itching to start or purchase. For the first time in my life, I contemplated the "r" word. I had never thought about retirement; with my addiction to work, retirement is tantamount to surrender. It was a frightening prospect for me. I even said it aloud to a few people — "Maybe it's time to retire and enjoy life a little" — to see how it would sound. It sounded terrible, but I didn't have any attractive options.

Little did I know that an unsolicited opportunity would usher me into a new phase of my career that, in some ways, would become the most satisfying.

14. THE TECH WHISPERER

My departure from Actronics sparked an article in the *Pittsburgh Post-Gazette* indicating I was retiring. I had floated that trial balloon mostly to see how I felt about it, to see if I could get comfortable with the idea of Jack Roseman, distinguished retiree. I could not, but I didn't have any promising alternatives.

About a week after the article ran, I got a visit from Mark Schneider of the Northside Civic Development Council, a community-based organization that was creating public-private partnerships to revitalize neighborhoods on Pittsburgh's Northside. Mark indicated Northside Civic was developing a business incubator in a refurbished brewery. Penn Brewery actually would produce beer, a new microbrew called Penn Pilsner. More importantly, the start-up businesses that would share the brewery's office space until they could stand alone needed counsel from an experienced entrepreneur.

"Would you consider being our in-house mentor?" Mark asked. "You wouldn't have to work more than one day a week. That's all we could afford."

"I know myself well enough to know that I could never limit my time to one day a week. I'd be there every day, even if you were paying me for one day only. No thanks."

Mark kept after me and wore down my resistance. And I can't deny that the idea of helping young entrepreneurs appealed to me. I'd always enjoyed teaching; mentoring is teaching in another form.

"I would need an office," I warned him.

"You got it."

Before we formalized the arrangement, I needed the blessing of two other Northside Civic executives: Tom Cox, the executive director, and Linda LeFever, an organizer and developer.

We all gathered at a Northside restaurant. I figured that the deal was pretty much done and that this lunch meeting was a formality. I know Mark and Tom also thought that; somewhere along the line, they forgot to tell Linda.

"Jack," she said, "what I'd really like to know is this: What's the biggest mistake you've ever made?"

My jaw dropped. She was treating me like a job candidate, not a senior executive being urged to (largely) volunteer his time. Tom and Mark were looking daggers at her. I fumbled around for an answer, all the while thinking: No one's ever asked me that before. I've interviewed thousands of job candidates, and I've never asked it before. Yet it's a good question. I'll add it to my repertoire.

As I was trying to tiptoe across that minefield, Linda asked me another question that came out of the woodwork. I flubbed this one, too.

After the meeting, Tom and Mark apologized profusely, but I cut them short.

"Apology not needed," I said. "Those were legitimate questions."

It was a bizarre meeting, but it didn't prove a deal-breaker. I signed on as in-house mentor and became great friends with Linda, Mark and Tom.

*   *   *   *   *

I loved my job. Just as I predicted, I was at my office in the brewery just about every weekday, working with a variety of fledgling businesses. A few had just the right formula, quickly outgrew the incubator and became successful concerns employing many people. One of those was a company called Guidance Technologies, which attracted "private placement" investment and thrived — at least for a while.

Most of the entrepreneurs at the brewery, however, were destined to fail, with or without my advice. Successful entrepreneurship requires many attributes — vision, passion and determination chief among them. In most cases, at least one of those characteristics was missing. I would say that the greatest number of these aspiring entrepreneurs ended up as consultants rather than operators of bustling businesses.

Although I was officially the mentor for these start-ups, I think I learned as much from them as they did from me. Not all the lessons were pleasant, either. I remember counseling one entrepreneur, a young African-American woman who had launched a travel agency and was concerned that racism in the business world might stifle her chances for success. When other black entrepreneurs voiced the same concerns, I decided to give a little presentation for them.

"You may find racism in the world outside this incubator," I lectured. "But when you're in business, there's only one color that matters: green. Show people you can make money for them and they won't care what color you are. I don't want to hear anything but green."

My young travel agency founder took me at my word and set out to conquer the business world. After a successful start, she thought she was ready to rent office space in Shadyside, one of Pittsburgh's trendier neighborhoods. The building owner agreed to the deal over the phone, but when he saw my friend in person, he advised her that the space had just been rented. Several days later, she drove by the building and noticed that the "For Rent" sign still was posted. Pretty clear what happened there.

Then, when she needed to staff up, she ran newspaper ads for help. She got a phone response from an enthusiastic candidate and set up an interview with her. When the candidate arrived and saw her prospective boss, she headed for the door.

"I would never work for a nigger," she said.

When my friend related all this to me, I was ashamed of my lack of sensitivity. Green is *not* the only color that counts in business. How could I have been so naïve to think otherwise?

I mentored for Northside Civic for about two years until personnel changes made the job less appealing. Tom Cox left the organization for a similar position in Cleveland but returned to Pittsburgh when his close friend, Tom Murphy, was elected the city's mayor. Cox served as Murphy's executive secretary and as chairman of the Urban Redevelopment Authority of Pittsburgh. We still meet regularly for lunch. Tom has achieved much as an urban developer, yet he's still managed to follow the principles of his training as a minister. He's one of the most interesting people I know.

Mark Schneider transitioned to the private sector and played an important role in many real estate projects, including the redevelopment and rebranding of Washington's Landing, site of an abandoned meat rendering plant. He also served a stint as chairman of the Sports & Exhibition Authority of Pittsburgh and Allegheny County. It pains me deeply to report that Mark and Linda LeFever died many decades prematurely. I lost a pair of good friends whom I loved dearly, and Pittsburgh lost a pair of its most committed, honorable developers.

* * * * *

While I was still at the brewery, I was approached by Jack Thorne, a professor of entrepreneurship at Carnegie Mellon University (CMU). I first met Jack when he served on the board of On-Line Systems and knew him as a highly respected authority on entrepreneurship — and a pretty successful dealmaker. He asked me to assist him with a large graduate class, which I was happy to do. Soon, my assistant's role blossomed. Jack offered me a position at CMU that would be somewhat similar to his. I would become a faculty member in the Graduate School of Industrial Administration — the formal name of the business school, which now is the Tepper School of Business — and would teach entrepreneurship to undergraduates and graduates as well as business leaders through CMU's executive program. We haggled a little about my rank but eventually agreed that I would be an adjunct professor.

My work at the brewery rekindled my enthusiasm for teaching, but when I took the CMU position in 1988, I was pretty much starting from scratch— no textbook, no syllabus, no game plan. Thank goodness for Jack Thorne. To help reintroduce me to academe, he allowed me to sit in his class, review the textbooks he used and give occasional guest lectures. Between Jack's notes and the textbooks he recommended, I was able to put a course plan together. I read those textbooks carefully and found little in them that I hadn't learned in the business world. That gave me a tremendous feeling of confidence.

One of the keystones of my course was a business plan. I required all my undergraduate and graduate students to develop business plans, by themselves or in collaboration with one or two colleagues. This forced them to focus on all the elements that a successful start-up requires. I would re-enforce the message by stimulating them in class with questions designed to help them determine if they really were entrepreneurial timber. Do you have a unique idea? Do you have the passion to work that idea round the clock? Can you innovate? Can you manage a complex organization? How would you handle bankruptcy — would it kill you? I wanted students to turn the microscope inward and see what they were made of. To spark a spirit of entrepreneurship, I often posed a hypothetical situation to them:

"Let's assume you work for a multinational company, GE, say, for 10 years, and let's assume your average annual salary for that decade is $100,000. So you make $1 million. After 10 years, you decide you're not happy with the tradeoff. You say to GE, here's your $1 million back. Can you please return my 10 years? Can't get them back, can you? Why is that equation fair?"

I was trying to get them to think about their goals. Do you want to grind it out in the corporate world, polluted by politics as it is, or would you prefer all the risks, challenges and potential poverty of entrepreneurship? What will you do with your life — that's the thing that counts.

I posed other questions to students to force them to think about their most important goals. I would start with a simple one from the textbook: *Over the next three to five years, what do you hope to accomplish?* Next, I would spin out another hypothetical situation: *You're my age. You're on your deathbed. As you look back at your life, what is the one thing you did that you really feel good about?* Then I would present a more complicated situation: *You go for a physical. The doctor says, I have good news and bad news. The bad news is, exactly one year from today, you'll die.*

The good news is, for that one year, you'll feel no pain. Now, tell me how you'll spend that year.

Write these answers down for yourself, I would tell them, side by side on a single sheet of paper. When you read them, you'll get a strong sense of who you really are and what you really want to do. I invited students to share their answers if they wanted to; a surprising number did share them, and a couple of the responses were doozies. A Pakistani student said he would spend his last year trying to "convert the pope to Islam."

I looked for some indication in his face that he was joking, but he was dead serious.

"You'll see him married first," I said.

Another student, a young girl from China, also was kind enough to share how she would spend her final year.

"I would take every drug under the sun," she wrote, "and I would go to bed with every white man I could find."

Brother. If you're the supposedly wise old professor, how do you respond to that? I thanked her for her honesty and left it at that.

My sense of teaching is that students learn best what they learn themselves. You can dispense advice from On High, and students may or may not relate to it. A better approach to giving advice: ask probing questions. When students ask you questions, turn them around so they're forced to look inward, to their own experiences, for the answers.

If students came to me for advice on development or implementation of their business plans, here's how the conversation typically would go.

"I can't find any investors for my business."

"Does the market need the product?"

"My research tells me it does."

"If that's true, why wouldn't an investor climb aboard?"

"Maybe it's because I don't have a track record."

"What can you do about that?"

"Maybe I can find a partner with experience and a solid reputation."

I was the guide, leading students to consider all aspects of the problem as well as potential solutions. But they made the conclusions themselves. They'll remember those conclusions a lot longer than if I'd issued them in the form of a decree.

Apparently, this Socratic approach became well known on campus. Once, an advisor sent a student to me, a young man from India who wasn't in any of my classes. His problem wasn't directly related to business.

"Something's really been bothering me lately," he said. "There doesn't seem much point to life. You're born, then poof, you die. What's the difference what you do?"

"Let me ask you something," I said. "Is it true that some poor people die on the streets in New Delhi and some other big cities in India?"

"Yes, it is true."

"What can you do about that?"

"I don't know what you mean."

"What if you made it your goal to keep one or two of those people from dying? They live because of your help."

I don't want to suggest that, in the space of a short

conversation, I cured his malaise, but he left my office with a different perspective, thinking of others rather than himself.

When a local magazine published a profile of me recently, it called me the "Tech Whisperer," citing this technique of turning around questions so that students and young entrepreneurs are providing their own answers. I must admit: I like the nickname.

*　　*　　*　　*　　*

I had a number of roles and titles in my 13 years at CMU. The university hired me as an adjunct professor but soon promoted me to distinguished adjunct professor. I was named associate director of the Don Jones Center for Entrepreneurship, which was named for one of the region's most respected and successful venture capitalists. After a few years, they dropped "adjunct" from my title and named me a full professor. Finally, I was named the John R. Thorne Professor of Entrepreneurship, which closed the circle, in a way, since it was Jack Thorne who brought me to the university. All those fancy titles made me sound like a Big Man on Campus, yet I was frustrated in my efforts to bring entrepreneurship instruction to a wider audience.

My students were primarily in CMU's business school, although I also taught classes through the university's executive program that were geared to leaders of businesses already operational. I'm guessing I reached about 200 such executives in my years at CMU. For all that, I believed strongly that students in other CMU schools, most notably computer science and engineering, would benefit from entrepreneurship courses. At some point in their careers, many of those students would aspire to start businesses, but they weren't getting any grounding in entrepreneurship in the traditional curriculum.

I spent about a year making my case to the dean of computer science, who finally agreed to add my courses to the computer science curriculum. The School of Engineering signed on as well. Everything was a go . . . until the professor in charge of all undergraduate business programs rejected the plan. I fought him tooth and nail, but he wouldn't give an inch — and he couldn't give me a good reason for his opposition. What made this especially galling was that I had copied him on every e-mail I'd sent to computer science and engineering, and not once had he so much as hinted his opposition.

This wasn't the only time campus politics ensnared me, but I found this battle particularly wearying. There had to be a better way to help young entrepreneurs without all this pissing for turf.

* * * * *

Indeed, there was a better way. It came to me through my old friend Bill Newlin of the Buchanan Ingersoll (BI) law firm, who had represented On-Line Systems and me in our successful fight against those federal kickback charges and other, less urgent corporate matters. We had stayed close and now, as I was preparing to leave CMU, Carl Cohen, Bill's colleague at BI, approached me with a proposition: BI would provide an office for me, where I would preside as an in-house mentor. While the law firm would pay me, I could make my own arrangements with any clients I signed. In turn, my presence would help BI attract and serve young entrepreneurs. They'd even come up with a name for my little nook: The Roseman Institute.

The idea of mentoring appealed to me — I'd been doing that for about 15 years at the brewery and CMU — but there were several aspects of the proposal that I found troubling. I was afraid I would be expected to steer business to BI, which I couldn't do in good conscience. If young entrepreneurs needed legal advice, I wanted to be able to recommend the law firms that would be best for them. So we agreed that, in those situations, I might give clients a list of three law firms they should consider, and that BI certainly could be among them.

I also wasn't keen about having my name in the title of the business and asked if we could come up with an alternative. Oh Jack, they said, we're already producing the stationary and business cards.

So that's how The Roseman Institute was born. The institute became my vehicle for finding and serving clients; most were technology start-ups looking for advice on attracting investors, fine-tuning their business plans and engaging the right personnel, consultants and board members. I got a few referrals from Buchanan Ingersoll's lawyers. Still others learned of the institute through my many speaking engagements and the articles on entrepreneurship I wrote for the Pittsburgh Technology Council and the *Post-Gazette*. At times, when my clients reached the next levels of development, they asked me to help develop exit strategies, including selling their businesses.

When I provided such services to students during my years at CMU, I never charged them. My sense was, their tuition was covering any advice I might give them. But when for-profit businesses sought my counsel, it was more than appropriate to charge them for my services. What should my fee be? Buchanan Ingersoll's top attorneys were charging $4,000 per day. I set my fee a touch higher — $5,000 per day. I wanted it known that I was the most expensive person in the shop. It was an eye-popping number that got everyone's attention. If you think you're spending $5,000 per day for some guru's advice, you listen.

Pretty sharp, I thought, yet I got a painful lesson in fees from a client named Frank W, who owned a software company he wanted to sell. Frank had found a prospective buyer in Texas, but somehow, their discussions turned acrimonious and the deal went nowhere.

"I pissed him off, Jack, and now he won't talk to me," Frank told me. "Can you do something to revive this?"

So I set about mending fences. I phoned the guy and set up a meeting with him in Pittsburgh. Mustering all the charm I could, I turned him around and got him to agree to Frank's original asking price. I was elated and turned it over to the lawyers to hammer out the details. Then I got a call from Frank.

"I've been thinking," he said. "The business is doing great right now. Why do I want to sell it?"

The deal was off, and with it went my fee, which was based on the sale of the company. That changed the way I structured things. From then on, when I was engaged to help sell a business, I asked my client: "What is the minimum offer you would accept?" If I lined up a buyer at that price, my fee became due. If the deal eventually fell apart, that was unfortunate, but I had done my job.

*   *   *   *   *

In my years at CMU and the Roseman Institute, I read probably 500 business plans and served as a consultant, advisor, board member or sales broker for more than three dozen companies. They're an interesting mix. Here's a sampler of some of my more memorable clients:

Perhaps the most dazzling success story of any of my clients or students is that of **Michael Kobold**, the son of a wealthy German industrialist. Young Mike launched his company, which crafted high-end watches, as a 19-year-old student at CMU. He took my entrepreneurship class, and, as all my students, was assigned development and submission of a business plan. Since he already had his company up and running, he figured the business plan would be a piece of cake.

When I reviewed his plan for selling watches on-line — at $1,000 to $5,000, no less — I found it preposterous. Here was a rich kid looking for a hobby, and I told him just that.

Mike, however, persisted — and he engaged me as an advisor. Today, his business, Kobold Watch Co., is headquartered in the Amish Country north of Pittsburgh, with operations in Pittsburgh and Katmandu, Nepal, where Kobold's high-tech watches are extremely popular with mountain climbers. The company sells about 1,000 watches per year. Oh yes. They're now priced at $10,000 apiece. So much for my advice.

Mike's watches have become must-have in certain circles. The late James Gandolfini, of *The Sopranos* fame, presented members of the production staff with Kobold watches to show his appreciation, and he was featured in a print ad for Kobold. It was a full-page ad — I advised Mike that anything less than a full page would make the company look small.

Yet Mike's finest hour came in 2015, after Nepal was devastated by an earthquake. He dropped everything he was doing, flew to Nepal and provided important assistance during the cleanup and rebuilding.

Mike still calls me for advice on his major business decisions. Once, when he was interviewed about me, Mike called me "a perfect mix between Father Christmas and Yoda." I hope that's a good thing because I have no idea what it means. I think it must be complimentary, though, because a few years ago, he presented me with a Kobold watch. I wear it with great pride. The only problem: it lacks an audible alarm feature, so I'm no longer able to set my watch alarm to go off each midnight, as I'd done since my heart attacks, to remind me that I'd been blessed with another day.

High tech my ass.

*   *   *   *   *

Perhaps the most important company I counseled was Agentase, a business that was co-founded in 1998 by **Keith LeJeune**. What made Agentase so special? It developed tools to detect hazardous chemicals. These capabilities are useful in industrial environments, of course, but they're also of considerable value to the U.S. Department of Defense in the detection of chemical or biological attacks.

Keith called on me shortly after launching Agentase and hired me as a consultant. I worked with him through the 2005 sale of the company to Wexford Capital. Following the transaction, Keith signed on as senior vice president of research and innovation for Allegheny Health Network. Agentase passed to several new owners and most recently was integrated into FLIR Systems, Inc.

*   *   *   *   *

One of my most successful relationships, both financially and personally, was with **Bill Mariotti**, a former student of mine who founded and owned Omega Systems, an application development and software consulting company. Omega boasted its own headquarters building near the University of Pittsburgh and CMU, a terrific location. Bill hired me as a consultant for Omega, then asked me to serve as chairman. This was no ceremonial role, as Bill had something specific and challenging in mind — the sale of his company.

"Jack," he said, "I want you to handle the sale. I'll give you a nice percentage if you're successful, but at the end of the day, I need x million in my pocket. That would make me happy."

"Fair enough," I said. "Let me ask you this. Are there any companies that have contacted you over the years about acquiring Omega?"

He mentioned only one: Keane, Inc., a $600 million computer services business that was based in Boston and traded on the American Stock Exchange. So this was the approach we developed: We would hire a broker to identify prospects, but I would handle the pitch to Keane myself.

It sounded great. Then Bill hit me with an "Oh by the way."

"Oh by the way," he said. "I promised my key employee that if she sticks with us through the sale, she'll get $500,000. I expect you to pay half."

This was not part of our original terms; the more I thought about it, the more it pissed me off. But the stakes here were substantial, and I didn't want this new wrinkle to be a deal breaker.

I called Keane to get the ball rolling — not a textbook cold call, like the time I got through to Jell-O's CFO from a phone booth in Dover, but it wasn't far off. Nevertheless, Keane was interested. After some initial resistance — they wanted Omega but not the Omega Building — we reached an agreement. Keane would purchase Omega, real estate and all, for a seven-figure sum. Further, they agreed to provide Mariotti's key employee with $500,000 over and above the sale price.

It was a great deal for all involved. Bill got his x million and then some. His loyal employee got her $500,000. Roseman did okay, too. As for Keane, it continued to grow and eventually was acquired by a unit of NTT Group, Japan's national phone company. Bill retired shortly after the sale and went on to perform valuable work for the Service Corps of Retired Employees (SCORE) and other nonprofits. Judy and I still play bridge with the Mariottis.

* * * * *

When **Sue Parker** needed an exit strategy for her software start-up, Paragon Systems, she asked me to help identify a buyer and facilitate Paragon's sale.

"I think we can find a buyer," I said. "What price are you thinking?"

She responded immediately.

"X million."

"We can get more than that."

"No. I've thought this through, Jack. I think Paragon is worth x million tops. I'd be happy with x million."

"Okay. That's what we'll do."

I sold Paragon for her asking price and brought Sue a little more money with a separate sale of Paragon's sister company. Sue was thrilled with the results. She retired from the business world, although these days, I think she's ready to get back in.

In my experience, Sue Parker is unique. I've never had another client say, "Get me x million and not a penny more."

* * * * *

As a student in my entrepreneurship class, **Sarjoun Skaff,** already had started his company, Bossa Nova Robotics, when he solicited my advice. His plan was solid, and I thought the market would welcome his product. I served on Sarjoun's board of directors, including a stint as chairman.

The company continues to thrive today, producing robots to help store employees keep track of inventory on their shelves, and I continue to help Sarjoun as a consultant. My association with Sarjoun is one of the longest-running relationships to emerge from my days at CMU — and it transcends business. When Sarjoun's parents visit from their native Lebanon, I always get together with them. Sarjoun calls me his "American Dad."

*   *   *   *   *

Most of my clients are in the tech sector, but that isn't always the case. In fact, I once advised an aspiring entrepreneur to abandon the tech sector for a more traditional business.

Craig Marcus was working in CMU's Computer Science Department while teaching computer programming and taking my entrepreneurship class. He submitted a plan, which I considered pretty good, for a cabinetry business.

"What do you suggest I do — stay in computer science or open up this company?" he asked.

"Open up the company."

"But my business plan shows that I won't make any more than $40,000 a year with the cabinetry business."

"Money is one type of reward," I said. "Job satisfaction is another. If cabinetry is what you really love, go for it."

He took my advice and opened his business. Was it the right decision for him? He thinks so. Today, through Marcus Studio in Pittsburgh's Larimer neighborhood, Craig designs, builds and sells exquisite furniture. As a way of saying thanks for my counsel, Craig built a beautiful desk for my office. He named his price, and I paid it. This was one time I had no intention of negotiating.

* * * * *

Not every idea bears fruit; not every start-up succeeds. I've counseled a number of businesses that failed. Each was a disappointment for me, none more so than the company envisioned by **Afshan Khan**, a Muslim from India who took my course as a grad student. Afshan wanted to start a business that would fill a void in the Muslim community — greeting cards for Muslim holidays.

That struck me as a terrific idea. I helped Afshan develop her business plan, and she entered it in an international business plan competition at the University of Texas; we flew to Austin together for the event. She won the contest, and she seemed to be off and winging.

Then, her father died, and Afshan felt obligated to take over his business, which manufactured ornamental plastic items for the home. She did well with the business for a while, but it nosedived and ultimately failed during the 2007-2009 recession. I still see Afshan from time to time, and we still talk wistfully about her Muslim greeting card idea.

* * * * *

My years as an entrepreneurship professor and mentor taught me that success is the intersection of talent, ambition and luck/timing, and that you usually need all three to succeed. Look at Afshan. There's no question that she had talent and drive aplenty. Luck? It wasn't there for her, and her great idea went unfulfilled.

You can't teach luck, but you can teach some of the other

elements of success. I tried to do that for the young men and women I counseled, and I'm gratified that so many of them succeeded. In a way, I helped give birth to a new generation of business leaders, then got to watch my "children" nurture the next generation. If that's what it means to be Father Christmas and Yoda, I'll take it.

15. WRITING THE BOOK ON ENTREPRENEURSHIP

To prepare for my courses at CMU, I read a number of textbooks on entrepreneurship; most were competent enough, but none really excited me. None of them made me want to drop what I was doing and start a business. I wondered if I could write and publish *that* book.

Over the years, I had written a number of articles about entrepreneurship for the *Pittsburgh Post-Gazette* and *TEQ*, the magazine of the Pittsburgh Technology Council. I wondered: if I put those articles together, write a few more to fill in any gaps, and work with an editor to smooth everything out, could that be the textbook I was looking for?

I bounced the idea off Steve Czetli, a fine writer and editor who served as a communications consultant for the tech council. First, he suggested, we needed to check with the tech council to get their take on who owned the rights to the articles I'd written. When the council confirmed that I owned them, Steve and I were in business.

We sat down in 2003 to write the book. With each chapter, I tried to offer words of advice illustrated by my personal business experiences. For a chapter on choosing associates wisely, for example, I included the cautionary tale about my old partner Saul Feldman, the man who cried from one eye. For a section on competing against well-established companies, I related my experiences at Heliodyne, when we snatched a company-saving NASA contract from the grasp of a very large company.

We called the book *Outrageous Optimism — Wisdom for the Entrepreneurial Journey*, with Steve as co-author. Even I wasn't outrageously optimistic enough to believe we could interest a mainstream publisher in the book, so Judy and I published it ourselves. We called ourselves Corbett Publishing, after my old elementary school in Lynn, and oversaw the production of 5,000 copies of the book.

*   *   *   *   *

Judy and I financed the entire press run — it wasn't cheap. Yet the book paid for itself, and then some, in a number of ways. Whenever I served as a guest lecturer or guest speaker, I referenced *Outrageous Optimism*, and I always had copies with me to sell. I used to tell people. "If you buy it and don't like it, I'll give your money back." No one ever asked for his money back. *Outrageous Optimism* opened quite a few doors for me.

Here's an example. On a plane heading from Boston to Pittsburgh, I sat next to a man who was reading a book on management. His name was Al Azadi, founder and president of Omix-ADA, a business that sells after-market equipment for Jeeps.

"Only for Jeeps?" I said. "That's not a business."

"I bought a house last week with no mortgage."

"Now *that's* a business."

I gave him my spiel about *Outrageous Optimism*.

"Buy the book, and if you don't like it, I'll double your money back."

I was upping the ante here, but I figured, what are the chances I'll hear from Al Azadi again?

About a month later, I did hear from him, by phone.

"Jack," he said, "this is the best business book I ever read. I want to hire you as an advisor.

"I don't travel for business. To that extent, I'm retired."

"How about if I come to Pittsburgh once a month, and we get together?"

He did just that, meeting with me in Pittsburgh once a month for a year. I counseled Al on the whole range of business matters. He was so grateful that, for many years, he sent us a Christmas gift every year. Once, he persuaded me to speak at a conference on after-market products. The seminar was in Las Vegas, and Al's company picked up all expenses for Judy and me. My presentation was such a hit that they posted it on YouTube. It didn't go viral, exactly, but you can view it on YouTube to this day.

Al didn't do badly, either. Omix-ADA grew to become the world's largest independent manufacturer of Jeep parts and accessories.

*   *   *   *   *

The late Jack Markowitz, former business editor of the *Tribune-Review*, wrote a favorable review of *Outrageous Optimism* — I think Steve persuaded him to read and consider the book — and a former student of mine, Manu Kumar, wrote a beautiful review for Amazon. Manu, by the way, practiced what I preached and went on to a successful career as an entrepreneur and venture capitalist. At K9 Ventures, the Silicon Valley fund he launched and operates, Manu calls himself "Chief Firestarter."

We sold *Outrageous Optimism* in many ways, in many venues. CMU bought bunches, at different times, for use as textbooks; Judy would pack up the books and hand-deliver them to campus. We sold a few through Amazon and Borders. Believe it or not, one of our most enduring markets was China, where my friend Tom Emerson, a venture capitalist and chaired professor at CMU, lectured at Peking University. Each year, we would ship about 100 copies to Beijing so that Tom's students could use them as textbooks. Peking University surmounted the language barrier by having one of its students translate *Outrageous Optimism* into Chinese.

Alan suggested that we put 100 copies aside — for our own use and posterity. We did that, and in time, those became the only unsold copies. We actually realized a profit on the book and were delighted to donate all the proceeds to a number of charities.

Our private stash of 100 dwindled over the years. If you wanted to buy a copy, I couldn't supply you with one, but I have seen them offered on-line for prices ranging from a penny to $2,000. I'm not sure what that says about the market.

Here are some excerpts that, I think, capture my approach to business through more than six decades:

Leadership:

" . . . you can't lead or motivate people until you understand yourself. Many people are born, live their whole lives fooling themselves, then die. An entrepreneur cannot afford to do that . . . If you understand yourself, you will be able to trust yourself — and that's a big part of being a successful entrepreneur. You need to be able to trust your instincts. But not to the exclusion of what the smart people around you are saying."

Competition:

"If you say there is no one doing what you want to do, no one solving that problem, the first thing I have to ask is whether it's a problem worth solving."

Persistence:

"Push yourself over the pest-line. It's probably further out than you think."

Ugly babies:

"Entrepreneurs are more like parents. They always tend to think their baby is beautiful . . . The advice I give to entrepreneurs is, if they really want an opinion on how beautiful their baby is, go to the top venture capitalists who invest in their type of venture and ask them for money . . . that's where you'll get the best judgments on just how beautiful your baby actually is."

Walking away:

"It takes both a passionate entrepreneur and a receptive marketplace to succeed. Walk away only when one or the other is missing."

Boards of directors:

"At many of the larger corporations, boards become rubber stamps for management. This isn't good for those companies, but for a start-up, a board without backbone can be fatal. You genuinely need smart advisors, savvy in your industry, who are willing to share their candid opinions and ask you hard questions."

Decision-making:

"The worst thing a leader or manager can demonstrate to the people around him or her is that he or she can't make a decision. So sometimes even a wrong decision is better than no decision or a delayed decision."

This, too, shall pass:

"When things are going great, don't be too happy because things will go lousy again. And when things are going lousy, don't be too sad because things will go great again. That's life and that's entrepreneurship . . ."

Hiring:

"A major issue in a company is: Do people enjoy working with the people around them? One of the first questions you should be asking when you hire people is, "Would this person be fun to work with?""

Work-life balance:

"Who you are to an organization is only a part of who you are. Who you are as a parent, a citizen, a neighbor or a friend is also important. It's all these things together that determine who you are as a human being. That is the judgment that counts."

Negotiating:

"A cardinal rule of negotiating is that the first one who blinks loses. That's why you always have to be willing to walk away. It's also why you have to mean what you say and be willing to stand by it, and you cannot blink."

Optimism:

"They say an optimist sees a glass of water half full instead of half empty. An entrepreneur looks at that same glass of water and because he or she is an outrageous optimist, sees a crystal goblet of wine."

16. THE DREAM (REVISITED)

As I write this, I've just celebrated my 85th birthday. It's an interesting and fascinating thing for me to be this age. I sometimes feel I live on a planet 20,000 light years away and now just a visitor here on earth. What do I see? Ants. Ants running this way, ants running that way. I don't feel any need to run with the ants. Since my first heart attack, I've lived 43 years with "one day to live." If I die today, no one owes me a thing. There's nothing more I need to accomplish. My bucket list? A blank sheet of paper.

Yet I surprise myself daily by remaining engaged. Several times each week, I lunch at Café Sam, a popular Shadyside restaurant, or Rico's in the North Hills and meet with clients, former students, friends and entrepreneurs I helped get started. Every so often, I meet with a new business prospect. I've stayed in touch with so many people over the years; seeing them brings me a tremendous amount of satisfaction. When I interact with them, I'm no longer looking at my life through a telescope. I'm fully engaged and still making personal history. If you're in the vicinity of Café Sam, stop in. You'll find me at my usual spot, Table 32.

Another form of engagement: I have this strange, inexplicable fondness for waitresses and waiters, an addiction that began way back in my days at HoJo. I like to help them, tease them, flirt with them, "adopt" them. I even have this line that I use. When a cute waitress serves me, I say, "I'm from Boston, and in Boston, there's a certain tradition that if you like your waitress, you have to hug her." Corny, right? But I've never had a waitress say no. When I hug them, it makes my day, and I think it's uplifting for them as well. They're not anonymous "servers" anymore because I've taken the time to get to know them.

Now that I have the time to look back at my life and ponder its many twists and turns, I think that deep and lasting engagement with others is one of the two great themes. The other is my rise from grinding, pervasive poverty and anti-Semitism to positions of respect in the corporate and academic worlds. If you were a Hollywood screenwriter trying to write a script of my life — you might call it *From Nobody to Somebody* or *From Poverty to Professor* — you would review the assorted trauma: brother murdered by Nazis; family so poor even the poor considered them Untouchables; held out of school because he couldn't speak English; denied affection by his mother, exceedingly introverted because he was certain he was ugly; scarred by anti-Semitism; bleeding ulcer in his 20s, life-threatening heart attack at 42. And you would say, "Nah, too improbable. Nobody could overcome all that. Didn't happen."

But it *did* happen. And if it happened to me, it could happen to others. One of the reasons I want to chronicle my life is to show others trying to break out of poverty that it's possible to beat the long odds. If there are other Rosemans — white, black or other — languishing in ghettos, I want to show them that escape is possible, and I want to point them in the right direction.

Amazing as my escape seems, the way I escaped is just as incredible to me. When I was plagued as a child by that recurring dream — Ma encouraging me to jump from a landing, then abandoning me, alone and injured, at the bottom of the stairs — I determined that I could count on no one, that my wits, my determination and my work ethic would be my only allies. Yet at every step of my career, I had support from loving family and wonderful colleagues who encouraged me and genuinely had my best interests at heart.

When Shari went away to college, and even later when she began her career in Maryland, she used to call home frequently. Every time I talked to her, she ended the conversation by saying, "I love you, Dad." I would just mumble because I couldn't say it, "I love you," in return. I was so angry with myself for this failing. How many times can you mumble unintelligibly? What's so hard about saying "I love you?" But I never heard it as a child, never said it as a child, and I found it impossible to express the love I felt. Now, I say it easily, but I couldn't then, not in those days.

Judy and our children taught me how to express love. Since childhood, I've believed that serving others is my purpose on earth; my family taught me how to do it. In turn, I would say to my children and grandchildren: Whether or not you believe in God is unimportant, but if you want to love God, you must love his children first. Be kind, friendly and truthful, be a compassionate steward of the animal kingdom. But love yourself — and forgive yourself — as well. Good times, bad times—they all pass. What remains is how you've treated the creatures of this earth.

Sei a mensch. That was my father's parting advice for me, and it's my wish for you as well. Believe me, it's not as simple as it seems.

*　*　*　*　*

Hy died in his 60s, but Lena stayed healthy into her 90s. She and her husband Joe never left Lynn. They raised their kids, Roberta and Eddie, in a second-floor apartment that, like Lena, began to show signs of age. Her hearing failed, and her legs swelled so that she needed a walker to get around. As her health deteriorated, she became essentially homebound. In fact, there was a period of several years where she left the apartment only once — for an emergency trip to the hospital. But her mind was sharp, and she maintained her sense of humor. Near the end, she had to move to a nursing home. When Roberta called to tell us Lena had died, she said all the staff at the nursing home marveled at Lena's sense of humor. It didn't surprise me. She had survived a harrowing transatlantic journey alone as a teenager and landed in America without knowing a word of English. How could she have made it without a sense of humor?

Alan's work took him to the Boston area on occasion, and he stopped to see Lena several times while her health was still good. I was pleased that he wanted to spend time with his aunt. I joined him once in Lynn, and we visited Lena together. Later, when Alan and I were back in our hotel, my son scolded me.

"Dad, I'm very surprised at you," he said. "That house needs a painting. The ceiling is falling down. The wallpaper is filthy. How can you let your own sister live this way? You have enough money to help, and I know you're generous."

I tried to defend myself.

"I just don't think she views the apartment as you see it. She's been living there a long time. That's her place. If I offered to pay for repairs, I think I'd be insulting her."

Alan and I rarely argue, so his rebuke stung. I thought about his suggestion and decided I would take a chance the next time I was at Lena's.

"I think the ceiling could use a paint job," I told her. "How about I call in somebody to do it? I'd be happy to pay for it."

Just as I'd feared, Lena got upset.

"There's nothing wrong with the ceiling," she said. "And if we do fix it up, the landlord will raise our rent."

Roberta and Eddie were just as adamant: the apartment was fine as it was. I never raised the issue again.

*   *   *   *   *

During one of my last visits, Lena, her children and I were chatting, and the subject of Leibel came up. I never got to know him, of course, but Lena had known her older brother, so her sense of loss must have been even greater than mine.

"Leibel and I had different fathers," she said. She continued in that same, matter-of-fact voice. "And my father was not your father."

"Wait. What are you telling me?"

"I'm telling you that Ma had three different husbands — Leibel's father, my father, and Abraham, the father of you and Hy. Ma's first two husbands died. She once showed me a picture of my real father."

I looked at my niece and nephew. Their faces were impassive, a pretty good indication that this bombshell to me wasn't news to them. Lena had shared it with them but not with me and probably not with Hy, who almost surely would have told me. I tried to keep my composure while I digested the news.

Bessie Guz, cold, reproving Bessie Guz, who never praised, hugged or kissed her children, was the last of the red-hot Ukrainian Jewish lovers? Could this really be true? I know Lena believed it, if only because she had seen a photo of her real father. But why did she wait until I was 83 years old to tell me? I realized then just how private Lena was, how her difficult life had forced her to protect herself, in part by keeping secrets. The funny thing was, I used to think that, because we kids were separated by so many years, Ma might have been fooling around. Who knew how close to the truth

I was?

Over the next few days, I tried to sort out my feelings about Lena's revelation. I was surprised my mother never told me, as close as we became late in her life; she had, after all, disclosed it to Lena. I also developed new respect for my father, who paid for Lena's passage to America, took her in and raised her when he didn't have a nickel to spare. He was supposed to be the dummy in the family. Maybe so, but when it came to generosity and kindness, he was the tops. Yet he never told me that Ma had two husbands before him. Perhaps he would have been embarrassed to admit he was Husband No. 3, or perhaps he thought his kids would bear a stigma if the world knew.

No matter how many different ways I looked at it, I couldn't deny that I was pissed off no one told me the Great Family Secret until I was in my 80s. Not angry so much as disappointed. Lena didn't tell me the truth. Ma didn't tell me the truth. Pa didn't tell me the truth. I've never been able to tolerate a liar, and my family lied to me. You might say, they didn't lie to you, they just didn't tell you everything, and let them off on a technicality. I don't buy that. If you really love someone, you don't hide the truth. How can you say, "I love you," and then conceal an important truth from the person you supposedly love? That's a foreign concept to me.

Despite my disappointment, my love for my parents is undiminished. My love for Lena, and the idea of what Leibel might have meant to me had he survived, is as strong as ever. Brother? Half brother? Sister? Half sister? Insignificant distinctions as far as I'm concerned. I accept it all now with the unconditional warmth for my family, for humanity in general, that eluded me as a young man.

"Don't rely on anybody," my dream mother lectured me. I

took that counsel to heart and was sure that, as I worked to make Roseman a household name, I would depend solely on my own strength and savvy. I achieved much of the success I craved . . . but only because beloved family and dear friends helped me each step of the way.

Now, when I think of that dream, I interpret it somewhat differently:

If you're standing on the precipice of a major business decision, whether it's starting a company or taking a job, and you're wondering if the risks are worth the potential gain — jump! The conditions never will be perfect for that next step; big gain always requires big risk. Now may be the time to do it.

If you fear that you may not have the support from family, friends and associates to help you overcome life's obstacles — jump! So what if it turns out no one has your back. You'll still have your native talents, and you'll have learned something important about the road ahead . . . and about yourself.

If you're pondering a leap into the uncertainties of life, and you're worried that you'll have to go it alone — jump! You may find people, wonderful people like Judy Rosenthal, Laura, Alan, Shari and Hy Roseman, Juste Maurice, Dominic Laiti, John Godfrey, Ted Barnett. *They'll* have your back, there to nurture and warm you and be nurtured and warmed in turn by the affection you provide. And when that happens, you'll have learned something even more important.

AFTERWORD

This memoir was extremely difficult for me to complete. For a person almost 86, I exercised my memory as best as I could. If my memory failed me at times — I sincerely hope it didn't—any mistakes were errors of inadvertence.

The surprising element of this endeavor is how many people, for whatever reason, gave me a helping hand, some knowingly, some not even suspecting they were my collaborators.

I started several times to list all the different people to whom I am indebted. The list grew so long that I had to scrap the idea for fear that I would omit too many people dear to me. So let me take this opportunity to thank the people who have had the biggest impact on my life.

My wife Judy, my children and their spouses, and my grandchildren have helped me in more ways than they could imagine. I am forever indebted to Judy, my wife of 57 years and my former student at the University of Massachusetts. Let me assure you: she has taught me more than she ever learned from me. Through love and commitment, I believe we've brought out the best in each other.

My children, Laura, Alan and Shari, grew to be wonderful people with wonderful families, although I'm not sure how much I had to do with that. When our kids turned 13, I gave them each a book by Wayne Dyer entitled *Pulling Your Own Strings*. I wanted them to think independently, and I thought the book would help. Today, each is a very different person, yet they're all independent thinkers. I love them dearly.

My mother and father gave me values that I have lived by — the value of the penny, work, education and integrity.

My brother Hy and my sister Lena helped me through a difficult childhood. Even though they were experiencing those same hardships, they always were there when I needed a pal, advice or support.

My five grandchildren — Sheena, Paige, Kyle, Brooke and Faylyn — have given me much joy and many new and surprising insights about life. I had hoped for a long time my kids would have kids. Sheena was the first, and she was born when I had wised up a little and become less preoccupied with work. Thus, when Sheena was growing, we became close. I'll never forget that period, probably one of the happiest of my life.

Most of my close friends over the years are gone, but my memories of them endure. Ted Barnett and I were close for many years. I miss our weekend trips to the bagel store, and I miss even more our long, spirited discussions that solved a lot of the world's problems. (For some reason, the world never recognized this achievement.)

I have fond memories of John Godfrey, founder of On-Line Systems and an ex-associate of mine at General Electric in Schenectady. John was the person responsible for my coming to Pittsburgh. We not only worked together, but we also became the kind of friends who could speak candidly to each other without fear of causing hurt.

Other close friends who helped shape and enrich my life: Dave Spitzer, my partner at Actronics; Bob Rosenthal, Judy's brother; Jack Tallan, Mike Rossin and Frank Rosenfeld, my gin rummy buddies; Jack Thorne and Don Jones, colleagues from my Carnegie Mellon University days.

And of course, Saras, my dearest friend who symbolically adopted me into her family so that I could introduce myself as a Jewish Brahmin. She and I had many, many discussions and yes, at times, arguments, to the enjoyment of both of us. I am extremely fond of her; she is probably the brightest person I know.

Since Carnegie Mellon University days, she has become an internationally renowned entrepreneurship guru.

For their help with this book, I'd like to extend special thanks to: Donna Silvia for being a joy to work with and for diligently attending to all the design details necessary for publication; Audrey Russo and Jonathan Kersting of the Pittsburgh Technology Council for their assistance and creativity in marketing the book;my good friends, Tom Cox and Bobby Feldman, for reviewing and critiquing the draft, and Evan Pattak, who nudged—sometimes cajoled — me to insights I might not otherwise have discovered.

A special word of thanks also to Dr. Jared Cohon, President Emeritus of Carnegie Mellon University. Jerry reviewed the draft meticulously and offered many suggestions we were pleased to implement. He gave generously of his time and talent; it's easy to see why he's so successful and respected.

I haven't even mentioned so many of the students, business associates and clients who grace the preceding pages because, as I say, I don't want to omit any who deserve my gratitude. If you have more loving family and friends than you could ever list, you've had a blessed life, indeed.